Burp Suite Essentials

Discover the secrets of web application pentesting
using Burp Suite, the best tool for the job

Akash Mahajan

BIRMINGHAM - MUMBAI

Burp Suite Essentials

Copyright © 2014 Packt Publishing

First published: November 2014

Production reference: 2111214

Published by Packt Publishing Ltd.
Livery Place
35 Livery Street
Birmingham B3 2PB, UK.

ISBN 978-1-78355-011-1

www.packtpub.com

Credits

Author
Akash Mahajan

Reviewers
Luca De Fulgentis
Rejah Rehim
David Shaw

Commissioning Editor
Anthony Albuquerque

Acquisition Editor
Harsha Bharwani

Content Development Editor
Neeshma Ramakrishnan

Technical Editor
Mrunal M. Chavan

Copy Editor
Sarang Chari

Project Coordinator
Rashi Khivansara

Proofreaders
Simran Bhogal
Ameesha Green
Lucy Rowland

Indexers
Monica Ajmera Mehta
Tejal Soni

Graphics
Abhinash Sahu

Production Coordinator
Manu Joseph

Cover Work
Manu Joseph

About the Author

Akash Mahajan is "That Web Application Security Guy." He has more than 10 years of experience in application and network security. Before starting his own company, he was a technical lead for one of the leading American commercial security software companies specializing in endpoint security. He then started working on the security of the web infrastructure for the Government of India.

He is the founder and community manager at null - The Open Security Community, where he has made major contributions in making null a national-level group and null Bangalore the biggest and most vibrant chapter.

He is currently a chapter leader of Open Web Application Security Project Bangalore (OWASP Bangalore).

He is the founder of The AppSec Lab, a company focused on application security, where he works with small- and medium-sized companies in securing their web server security, web security, and mobile security, and guiding them to stay secure while being competitive.

Currently, his areas of research include DevOps, SecOps, security in SDLC, cloud security, and security awareness through community building. He conducts a lot of training as well, including the extremely popular Xtreme Web Hacking.

He was actively involved with the Bangalore Barcamp Planners group and has organized events such as AppJam and MobileCamps all over India, where he has evangelized security to small- and medium-sized enterprises.

Acknowledgments

I would like to thank my parents for their constant guidance and encouragement. They gave me all the independence in the world to break rules and question fundamentals and have fun while doing all that. I also want to thank my wife, Lubaina; finding someone like her to be with me and agree to marry me rekindled my faith in fate and destiny. She takes care of the house and all my tantrums with a brilliant smile all the time. I want to thank my elder sister, who has the unshakeable faith in my abilities that only elder sisters can have. Apart from my family, I would like to thank my friends Riyaz and Anant whom I met at null - The Open Security Community and who are far more brilliant and knowledgeable than I will ever be.

I would like to thank Neeshma, whose help, support, and eternal patience in dealing with me is the only reason this book was completed. I would like to thank the technical reviewers, David Shaw, Luca De Fulgentis, and Rejah Rehim, who read through all that I wrote—most of which in the first draft was pretty sad. They guided me to make this book much better than I ever imagined it could be. Their insights and comments helped me understand and correct numerous mistakes and blunders. I will always be grateful to them for giving their time and effort to this endeavor.

About the Reviewers

Luca De Fulgentis is an Offensive Security enthusiast with experience in application security engineering and penetration testing. He holds a Master's degree in Computer Engineering from Politecnico di Milano, from where he graduated with a thesis on evolutionary fuzzing. As the CTO of Secure Network S.r.l., he delivers and coordinates the company's top-notch security services. He is also involved in training tigers for the team and researching advanced client-side exploitation techniques, cross-device attacks, and Windows Phone platform security.

Rejah Rehim is currently a software engineer with Digital Brand Group (DBG), India, and is a longtime preacher of the open source community. He is a steady contributor to the Mozilla Foundation, and his name has been featured in the San Francisco Monument made by the Mozilla Foundation.

He is a part of the Mozilla add-on review board and has contributed to the development of several node modules. He has also been credited with the creation of eight Mozilla add-ons, including the highly successful Clear Console add-on that was selected as one of the best Mozilla add-ons of 2013. With a user base of more than 44,000, it has registered more than 450,000 downloads till date. He has successfully created the world's first, one-of-a-kind, open source, Linux-based security penetration testing browser bundle, PenQ. It is preconfigured with tools for spidering, advanced web searching, fingerprinting, and much more.

Rejah is also an active member of OWASP and the chapter leader of OWASP Kerala. He is also one of the moderators of the OWASP Google+ group and an active speaker at Coffee@DBG, one of the most premier monthly technology reviews in Technopark, Kerala. Besides being a part of the Cyber Security division of DBG currently and QBurst in the past, he is also a fan of process automation and has implemented it in DBG.

David Shaw has extensive experience in many aspects of information security. Beginning his career as a network security analyst, he monitored perimeter firewalls and intrusion detection systems in order to identify and neutralize threats in real time. After working in the trenches of perimeter analysis, he joined the External Threat Assessment Team as a security researcher, working closely with large financial institutions to mitigate external risk and combat phishing attacks.

David joined Redspin in 2009 and has worked as a senior security engineer, director of penetration testing, and senior director of engineering. He is currently the CTO and Vice President of Professional Services at Redspin, specializing in external and application security assessments and managing a team of highly skilled engineers.

He has keen interest in complex threat modeling and unconventional attack vectors and has been a speaker at THOTCON, NolaCon, ToorCon, LayerOne, DEF CON, BSides Las Vegas, BSides Los Angeles, and BSides Seattle.

www.PacktPub.com

Support files, eBooks, discount offers, and more

For support files and downloads related to your book, please visit www.PacktPub.com.

Did you know that Packt offers eBook versions of every book published, with PDF and ePub files available? You can upgrade to the eBook version at www.PacktPub.com and as a print book customer, you are entitled to a discount on the eBook copy. Get in touch with us at service@packtpub.com for more details.

At www.PacktPub.com, you can also read a collection of free technical articles, sign up for a range of free newsletters and receive exclusive discounts and offers on Packt books and eBooks.

https://www2.packtpub.com/books/subscription/packtlib

Do you need instant solutions to your IT questions? PacktLib is Packt's online digital book library. Here, you can search, access, and read Packt's entire library of books.

Why subscribe?

- Fully searchable across every book published by Packt
- Copy and paste, print, and bookmark content
- On demand and accessible via a web browser

Free access for Packt account holders

If you have an account with Packt at www.PacktPub.com, you can use this to access PacktLib today and view 9 entirely free books. Simply use your login credentials for immediate access.

Table of Contents

Preface

This book on Burp is meant for web security testers. You might be using browser plugins or automated scanners or even other interception proxy tools. In this book, you will see how Burp Suite is a versatile tool that allows almost any kind of web security testing based on your needs. This book will build on how Burp can be used with upstream proxies, SSL certificates, and more. You will learn how to search, extract, and do pattern matching for requests and responses and use that knowledge to test complex and simple web applications. You will learn to use different tools and components together to form a powerful chain of tools for web testing. As a professional tester, we need to be able to report our work, safeguard it, and sometimes even extend the tools that we use.

You will learn how different components of Burp Suite can be used together and how to use Burp Suite like a pro. You will learn to embrace the user-driven workflow for testing web applications. You can customize and extend Burp according to your needs for maximum testing and minimum software.

This book has an easy-to-follow style, where we focus on understanding what the problem is that we are trying to solve and how Burp can make it easy for us to solve. Looking at scenarios, real-world use cases, and applying the philosophy of how Burp is designed makes for an easy read and a highly actionable list of items for you to take back to your workplace.

What this book covers

Chapter 1, Getting Started with Burp, starts with an introduction to Burp Suite. We will cover some of the advanced flags that can be passed to the software when we invoke it from the command line. By the end of this chapter, you will have a pretty good idea of running Burp Suite in various operating systems, while being able to tweak it for maximum performance.

Chapter 2, Configuring Browsers to Proxy through Burp, explains that interception proxies work best when used with a browser software. Even though it is quite simple to get Burp working with a browser, advanced users can use additional browser extensions to perform powerful and customized integrations. By the end of this chapter, you will have configured your browser to use Burp as an interception proxy. Additionally, using browser extensions, you will create a powerful chain of tools to perform web security testing.

Chapter 3, Setting the Scope and Dealing with Upstream Proxies, shows how more and more complex web applications are being tested, including the ones that run primarily on mobile platforms. How does one configure Burp Suite to intercept in such cases? Testing web applications available on the Internet is quite simple with Burp, but how do we test applications that are inside corporate networks, running on company intranets? By the end of this chapter, you will know how to work with SSH port forwarding, SOCKS-based proxies, and intercept HTTP traffic coming from mobile devices.

Chapter 4, SSL and Other Advanced Settings, teaches that SSL-enabled applications sometimes require additional configuration. Usually, you add the Burp Suite CA certificate to your browser and start testing, but sometimes this is not desirable or possible at all. Some additional settings make it possible for nonbrowser-based HTTP applications and thick clients to be tested. By the end of this chapter, you will be able to set up and test SSL-enabled applications without any errors. You will also be able to test thick clients or clients that are not proxy-aware.

Chapter 5, Using Burp Tools As a Power User – Part 1, shows that Burp Suite is powerful due to its amazing set of tools. We will start with Target, covering Site map and Scope, and then we will move to Proxy, which is the workhorse for testers. Then, we will move to the attack tool of choice, Intruder. After Intruder, we will cover the Scanner tool and discuss when we should use the Scanner tool. We will end the chapter with the Repeater tool, which supercharges the manual testing part by making it dead simple to repeat requests and see responses.

Chapter 6, Using Burp Tools As a Power User – Part 2, covers the other tools that make up the Burp Suite software and shows us how tools such as Spider, Sequencer, Decoder, Comparer, and Alerts work in sync to provide us with what we need to test web applications.

Chapter 7, Searching, Extracting, Pattern Matching, and More, explains that the suite of tools provided by Burp is quite powerful in terms of performing the heavy lifting of crafting HTTP requests and responses based on our actions on the web applications. An important aspect of this power is the ability to match, extract, find, grep, and search all the requests and responses based on our requirements. In this chapter, you will learn the various ways in which we can search, extract, and pattern match data in requests and responses, which allow us to complete our testing.

Chapter 8, Using Engagement Tools and Other Utilities, covers something called the engagement tools of Burp suite. These tools allow us to automate some of the more mundane and boring parts of the security testing process. Engagement tools is a Pro-only feature of Burp Suite. Apart from the engagement tools, we will look at some smaller utilities that aid the testing process such as Search, Target Analyzer, Content Discovery, Task Scheduler, CSRF PoC Generator, and Manual Testing Simulator.

Chapter 9, Using Burp Extensions and Writing Your Own, shows that not only does Burp Suite come with its own rich set of tools, but it also provides API interfaces to extend its functionality. Many security researchers have written extensions that enhance the native functionality or add to the already rich toolset. By the end of this chapter, you will be able to use Burp Extensions and even write a sample extension in Python.

Chapter 10, Saving Securely, Backing Up, and Other Maintenance Activities, states that Burp Suite is just like any other testing tool. As with any software, it is imperative that you make regular backups and carry out other maintenance activities. By the end of this chapter, you will have all the knowledge about ensuring that your Burp Suite data is backed up properly and securely and how you can run scheduled tasks for backup and other maintenance activities.

Chapter 11, Resources, References, and Links, provides a number of great resources and references that you can rely on. It provides you with the primary references that you should follow to get more insight into how web security practitioners use Burp. We will list useful and informative resources for application security as well.

What you need for this book

As this is a book about Burp Suite, we need Burp Suite. Most of the topics can be covered using the free version, but some of the topics require the Burp Suite Pro version.

To use Burp Suite, which is an application written in Java, we need the Java Runtime Environment. While Java 7 should suffice, the software will run okay with Java 8 as well.

To follow the steps and try out web security testing, we require a modern web browser, such as Mozilla Firefox, Google Chrome, Microsoft Internet Explorer, or others.

To try out Burp Extensions or attempt to write one would require Jython or JRuby based on the language you choose.

Who this book is for

This book is for anyone interested in learning how to use Burp Suite to test web applications.

If you have some experience of web security testing and Burp Suite as well but now would like to become proficient in using all the different tools and options present in Burp Suite so that your testing can become more powerful and effective, this is the book for you.

Conventions

In this book, you will find a number of styles of text that distinguish between different kinds of information. Here are some examples of these styles, and an explanation of their meaning.

Code words in text, database table names, folder names, filenames, file extensions, pathnames, dummy URLs, user input, and Twitter handles are shown as follows: "The official documentation cautions users from double-clicking on the .jar file."

A block of code is set as follows:

```
# Since we didn't get a request, we will look at response.
responseInfo = self._helpers.analyzeResponse(self._
helpers.bytesToString(messageInfo.getResponse()))
```

```
# Many times, we figure out next steps based on the status
code of the response.
self._stdout.println(responseInfo.getStatusCode())
```

Any command-line input or output is written as follows:

```
java -jar -Xmx2048M /path/to/burpsuite.jar
java -jar -Xmx2G /path/to/burpsuite.jar
```

New terms and **important words** are shown in bold. Words that you see on the screen, in menus or dialog boxes for example, appear in the text like this: "We need the JRE, so click on the **Download** button under **JRE**."

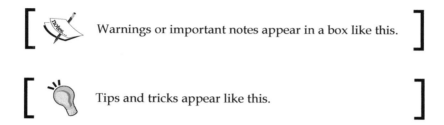

Warnings or important notes appear in a box like this.

Tips and tricks appear like this.

Reader feedback

Feedback from our readers is always welcome. Let us know what you think about this book—what you liked or may have disliked. Reader feedback is important for us to develop titles that you really get the most out of.

To send us general feedback, simply send an e-mail to feedback@packtpub.com, and mention the book title via the subject of your message.

If there is a topic that you have expertise in and you are interested in either writing or contributing to a book, see our author guide on www.packtpub.com/authors.

Customer support

Now that you are the proud owner of a Packt book, we have a number of things to help you to get the most from your purchase.

Errata

Although we have taken every care to ensure the accuracy of our content, mistakes do happen. If you find a mistake in one of our books—maybe a mistake in the text or the code—we would be grateful if you would report this to us. By doing so, you can save other readers from frustration and help us improve subsequent versions of this book. If you find any errata, please report them by visiting http://www.packtpub.com/submit-errata, selecting your book, clicking on the **errata submission form** link, and entering the details of your errata. Once your errata are verified, your submission will be accepted and the errata will be uploaded on our website, or added to any list of existing errata, under the Errata section of that title. Any existing errata can be viewed by selecting your title from http://www.packtpub.com/support.

Piracy

Piracy of copyright material on the Internet is an ongoing problem across all media. At Packt, we take the protection of our copyright and licenses very seriously. If you come across any illegal copies of our works, in any form, on the Internet, please provide us with the location address or website name immediately so that we can pursue a remedy.

Please contact us at copyright@packtpub.com with a link to the suspected pirated material.

We appreciate your help in protecting our authors, and our ability to bring you valuable content.

Questions

You can contact us at questions@packtpub.com if you are having a problem with any aspect of the book, and we will do our best to address it.

1

Getting Started with Burp

Burp Suite is a collection of tightly integrated tools that allow effective security testing of modern-day web applications. It provides a great combination of tools that allow automated and manual workflows to test, assess, and attack web applications of all shapes and sizes. Getting started with Burp is easy. With some application, we can become extremely comfortable and skilled at using the various powerful tools that are offered by Burp Suite.

Burp Suite is a piece of modern software written in the Java language. Java makes it cross-platform and extremely versatile for use both by novices and professionals. This chapter will get you started with Burp quickly while giving you enough information that will facilitate our journey of getting acquainted with Burp Suite. The tool, unlike point-and-click automated scanners, is meant to be used in a hands-on manner, and while it makes it easy to automate parts of the testing, a lot can be done by the tool in the hands of an expert. Since our aim is to optimize the way we use Burp, through this chapter, we will get to know a few tricks that will make it easy to start with.

Burp Suite is distributed as a single Java Archive (`.jar`) file. The free version can be downloaded from `http://portswigger.net/burp/downloadfree.html`. There is no registration or form to fill out, but if you'd rather get the Pro version, which I highly recommend, then you need to buy it from the same website to be able to download it. There are significant differences between the free version and the Pro version, but if you are a serious tester looking for the best value-for-money scanner / web application security tool, it should be Burp Suite Pro.

The main differences between the free version and the Pro version of Burp Suite are:

- Burp Scanner
- The ability to save and restore your work
- Engagement tools, such as Target Analyzer, Content Discovery, and Task Scheduler

These are the topics we'll be covering in this chapter:

- Starting Burp from the command line
- Setting memory options based on our requirement and system RAM
- Troubleshooting any IPv6 error that occurs sometimes

Oracle Java 1.6 or above is currently required for the software to run.

Oracle Java 1.6+ is usually installed for Windows and Mac OS X. If your computer doesn't have it installed, go to `http://java.com`, choose the version of **Java Runtime Environment** (JRE) for your operating system, and follow the installation instructions.

The official documentation cautions users from double-clicking on the `.jar` file. This is to ensure that we can clearly specify the amount of RAM allocated for the Burp process when we start it.

Some people have successfully run Burp with other flavors of Java, but for now, we will focus on running it well with Oracle Java 1.6 or above.

Starting Burp from the command line

Burp doesn't have an elaborate setup process. Starting Burp is as simple as executing a command in your shell of choice.

Starting Burp requires Java to be already installed and configured on your computer. If your computer doesn't already have Java 1.6+, you can get it for free from `http://www.oracle.com/technetwork/java/javase/downloads/index-jsp-138363.html`.

We need the JRE, so click on the **Download** button under **JRE**.

If your computer already has Java 1.6 or above installed, execute the following in your shell:

```
java -jar /path/to/burpSuite.jar
```

Those who have done Java programming will understand what is happening here. We are passing a JAR to the Java runtime. Please note there are no command-line options that need to be passed to Burp Suite.

Specifying memory size for Burp

If we start Burp Suite by double-clicking on the `.jar` file, the Java runtime will allocate the maximum memory available to Burp on its own. The total amount allocated might vary based on the available system RAM. Since Burp Suite will capture hundreds and sometimes thousands of requests and responses of various sizes, it makes sense to allocate memory when we start the program.

There is the possibility that Burp Suite might crash if the total memory available is not enough. While doing a security assessment, we don't want to worry about disruption in our work or the feeling that we may lose valuable data about the assessment due to Burp Suite crashing. Therefore, it is prudent to specify how much system RAM is allocated to Burp Suite in the beginning itself.

Specifying the maximum memory Burp is allowed to use

We can use command-line flags provided by Java to ensure that Burp has enough, and more, memory to use while running our security assessment:

```
java -jar -Xmx2048M /path/to/burpsuite.jar
java -jar -Xmx2G /path/to/burpsuite.jar
```

Both these commands will allocate 2 GB of RAM to Burp Suite. We can also pass options for gigabytes, megabytes, or kilobytes. You can read up more about this at the Oracle page at `http://docs.oracle.com/cd/E13150_01/jrockit_jvm/jrockit/jrdocs/refman/optionX.html#wp999528`.

This should be enough for most web applications that need to be tested. If you have more system RAM to spare, you can even increase it further. There is a small caveat you should know. If you increase the memory allocated to Burp Suite beyond 4 GB, the **Java Virtual Machine (JVM) garbage collector (GC)** will need to do more work. This has been known to adversely affect the performance of Java-based applications. Keeping that in mind, there are clear performance gains that can be achieved by increasing the minimum heap size from the default, which can be as low as 128 MB on older machines.

Ensuring that IPv4 is allowed

Sometimes, Java picks up the IPv6 address on the interface, and Burp is unable to make any connections to websites returning an IPv4 address. This results in a Java error, which is as follows:

java.net.SocketException: Permission denied

The browser also shows a cryptic error, which is as follows:

Burp proxy error: Permission denied: connect

If we ever encounter this error, all we need to do is tell Java that we want to use the IPv4 interface by passing the following parameter to the runtime:

```
java -Xmx2048M -Djava.net.preferIPv4Stack=true -jar /path/to/
burpsuite.jar
```

This command and flag tells the Java runtime that we will prefer the IPv4 network stack to run the Burp Suite JAR file. Another option is to set a Java option environment variable.

Please note that by running the preceding command, the IPv6 interface will be disabled.

Many people have reported this as a bug on the Burp support forums. Most of the people who complained were using Microsoft Windows 7 64-bit operating system running a 32-bit version of the JVM.

Working with other JVMs

The official documentation of Burp doesn't say anything about not working with JVMs apart from the official Oracle Java. There was a time when if we tried to run Burp Suite with OpenJDK, it would start off by giving a warning. But now, it runs perfectly without any warnings in Kali with OpenJDK.

Kali is a Linux-based distribution that has been specifically created for penetration testing and security testing of applications and networks. Previously, it was known as Backtrack. In the following screenshot, we can see that it runs the OpenJDK JRE and is able to run Burp Suite without any issues:

```
java.runtime.name           OpenJDK Runtime Environment
java.runtime.version        1.6.0_31-b31
java.specification.name     Java Platform API Specification
java.specification.vendor   Sun Microsystems Inc.
java.specification.version  1.6
java.vendor                 Sun Microsystems Inc.
java.vendor.url             http://java.sun.com/
java.vendor.url.bug         http://java.sun.com/cgi-bin/bugreport.cgi
java.version                1.6.0_31
```

Summary

We have successfully managed to start Burp Suite. Usually, we just double-click on the application shortcut and get it working. However, if you want to utilize the full power of the application, we need to understand some of the underlying concepts of memory and networking.

In this chapter, you learned how to allocate and reserve a specified amount of RAM for use while Burp Suite runs. This will ensure that while doing a security assessment, memory issues will not hamper our progress in any way. We also saw an error that can crop up, which is quite difficult to understand unless you have seen it before.

Now that we have successfully started Burp Suite, in the next chapter, we will see how to configure our web browsers to send web traffic through it for interception and analysis.

2
Configuring Browsers to Proxy through Burp

The Burp Suite Proxy tool is an intercepting proxy. An intercepting proxy intercepts all the traffic that is sent toward it from a client and all the resulting responses from the server as well.

The primary job of the Burp Suite Proxy tool is to intercept regular web traffic, which goes over **Hypertext Transfer Protocol (HTTP)**, and with additional configuration, encrypted HTTP (HTTPS) traffic as well. All of this to make it easy for you to see all interactions and data that goes to and come from the web server. If you can see what is happening in terms of requests and responses, you can test the website security using various techniques and approaches available to you.

Burp Suite can be used to intercept any client-server communication that goes over HTTP. The most common web clients are the web browsers that users like you and me use. There are other software capable of crafting and working with HTTP requests, such as curl and Wget.

Some desktop software that does send out HTTP requests don't have any provision to specify proxy information. Burp Suite allows you to intercept traffic from such clients using invisible proxying. We will cover this in detail in *Chapter 4, SSL and Other Advanced Settings*.

Note that although Burp Suite is a lot more than just a proxy, everything starts with configuring browsers to proxy through Burp Suite.

Let's see how we can configure Microsoft Internet Explorer, Google Chrome, and Mozilla Firefox to proxy all their web traffic through Burp Suite.

Configuring widely used browsers to proxy through Burp Suite

In this section, you will see how to configure commonly used browsers to proxy through Burp Suite.

Microsoft Internet Explorer

The following simple steps allow us to configure Microsoft Internet Explorer ready to be used with Burp Suite:

1. Start Microsoft Internet Explorer.

2. Click on **Tools** in the main menu bar.

3. Click on **Internet Options** and choose the **Connections** tab:

4. Click on **LAN settings**, as shown in the following screenshot:

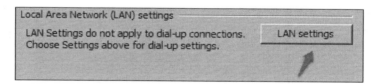

5. Check **Use a proxy server for your LAN**.

6. Add localhost as the hostname and 8080 as the port number, as shown in the following screenshot:

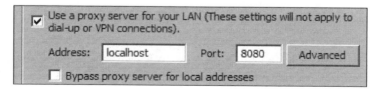

7. The address localhost and the port 8080 are the default values Burp Suite uses once it is started. You will have an opportunity to change this to something else later.

8. At this point, once you click on **OK**, you have successfully configured Microsoft Internet Explorer to use Burp Suite as your interception proxy server.

9. You can verify this by going to `http://burp` in your newly configured browser. You will see a welcome message on this page. If you don't see such a message, confirm that Burp Suite is running at this point. Take a look at the following screenshot:

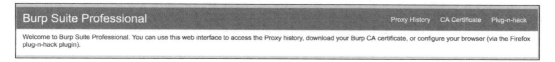

Google Chrome

Google Chrome picks up the system's proxy settings. If, for some reason, that doesn't happen, here is how you can quickly configure Burp Suite as the interception proxy in it:

1. Start Google Chrome.

2. Click on the icon that looks like three horizontal parallel lines, which is used to customize and control Google Chrome. This is present in the top-right corner of the browser window.

3. From the menu that opens up, click on **Settings**.

4. Another way to reach the **Settings** page is through a URL `chrome://settings/`. Type this in the address bar, and you should be able to see some settings.

5. Type `Proxy` in the search bar in the top-right corner, and you will get a button to change the proxy setting. Take a look at the following screenshot:

6. You will notice this opens the same dialog box as the Microsoft Internet Explorer browser; you can follow the same steps from 4 till 9 and configure the proxy settings.

Mozilla Firefox

Just like Google Chrome, if you have set the interception proxy settings properly in Microsoft Internet Explorer, then you are already all set. While this is great, if we don't care about sending all the HTTP traffic of the system to Burp Suite, this is a problem. With Mozilla Firefox, we can ensure that intercepting proxy configuration only sends browser-generated traffic to Burp Suite. This is one reason Firefox is preferred for the testing and security assessment of web applications. The next set of steps allows us to configure Mozilla Firefox so that it is ready for use with Burp Suite:

1. Start Mozilla Firefox.

2. Click on **Tools** in the main menu bar and choose **Options**.

3. Once the **Options** window opens, go to **Advanced | Network**, as shown in the following screenshot:

4. Add `localhost` in the **HTTP Proxy** textbox and `8080` in the **Port** text box:

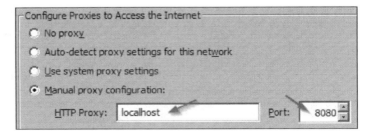

5. Now, all your HTTP traffic from Mozilla Firefox will go through Burp Suite.

6. By default, when Burp Suite starts, it starts with the intercept mode on. This means if you try to browse at this point, it would seem like nothing is happening. Behind the scenes, Burp Suite is in the interception mode and waiting for your input. At this point, you can either forward the request or switch off the intercept mode.

7. You can toggle the intercept mode, forward the request, or even drop it:

Fine-grained proxy configuration

Configuring the proxy every time for the entire browser is cumbersome. Additionally, configuring the proxy sets the proxy browser wide. Mozilla Firefox has a rich tradition of extending the core functionality using browser add-ons. We will use one such add-on to get fine-grained control over what traffic should be proxied.

FoxyProxy Standard is a Mozilla Firefox add-on to get fine-grained control over proxy traffic. It automates the processing of settings required to use proxies in Firefox. Using FoxyProxy is quite simple.

If you haven't used an intercepting proxy before with any browser, you might not understand the reason why we should use a browser-specific add-on to set up the proxy configuration, but if you are planning to regularly use interception proxies in your work flow, the initial time spent will become an invaluable time saver going forward.

There are multiple reasons to use the FoxyProxy Standard add-on. Primarily, it allows us to ensure that we only send selective traffic to Burp Suite. We can configure FoxyProxy in such a way that only the actual target website that we want to test is forwarded to Burp Suite and the rest of the traffic is sent directly.

Setting up FoxyProxy

Follow these steps to set up FoxyProxy:

1. Go to **Tools | Add-ons** in the main menu bar.

2. In the search box present in the top-right corner, type FoxyProxy Standard.

3. Click on the **Install** button present on the search results for FoxyProxy Standard.

4. Restart the browser after the add-on is downloaded and installed.

5. Once restarted, you will see a small fox icon next to the address bar within a red circle.

6. Right-click on that icon and choose **Options**.

7. Click on the **Add New Proxy** button present on the right-hand side, as shown in the following screenshot:

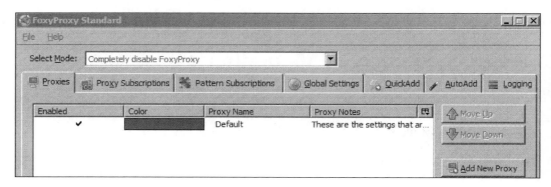

8. This opens a new settings window. There will be three tabs visible. Add the same values for **Host** and **Port** here as well.

9. Now click on the **URL Patterns** tab and add a new pattern. Add a new pattern name as example and an actual pattern as *example.com/*.

10. We also need to add a pattern name, Burp, and a pattern, *burp/*, for that. This is a special URL that is required for its working.

11. Now, we can click on **OK** to come back to the main **FoxyProxy Standard** window. In this window, we need to select the mode as **Use proxies as their pre-defined patterns and priorities**.

12. Click on the **Close** button, and we have successfully configured FoxyProxy Standard for our purposes.

A good professional tip is to give a different color to every proxy that we set up using FoxyProxy. Many times, we may want to run multiple proxies on our machines, and the colors will indicate which proxy the data is being sent to.

Mozilla Plug-n-Hack extension

Mozilla has an interesting configuration extension called Plug-n-Hack that Burp Suite supports out of the box. Even though it seems like a very cool idea and makes it easy for people starting with this kind of setup, the current setup is a little tricky to get going. Perform the following steps:

1. Download the add-on .xpi file from https://github.com/mozmark/ringleader.

2. We can trust this link because Mozilla has mentioned it in their blog post, https://blog.mozilla.org/security/2013/08/22/plug-n-hack/.

3. We can install the `.xpi` file using the Firefox **Add-ons** manager:

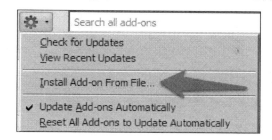

4. Once installed, go to the URL `http://burp/pnh` in a new tab.

5. Click on **Configure your browser** and enable the configuration after accepting the warning.

6. This has installed the proper configuration required for Burp Suite for use as an interception proxy and some more additional configurations related to SSL handling.

Exclusive Firefox profile

It is advisable to create a new profile to add FoxyProxy or the Plug-n-Hack extension rather than working in your primary profile. Mozilla Firefox has a handy profile manager, which can be invoked using a command-line flag, and you can use it to create a security testing profile very easily:

```
/path/to/firefox-binary -ProfileManager
```

After issuing this command, the following window will appear:

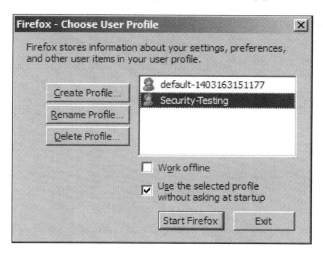

Summary

We successfully intercepted traffic from our browser to Burp Suite. This allows Burp Suite to see each and every request that leaves our browser. For our toolchain, we can use Firefox with the FoxyProxy Standard add-on and ensure that only selective traffic can be sent to Burp Suite. We also configured Internet Explorer, Chrome, and Firefox to proxy traffic through Burp Suite and now, we are ready to go ahead.

The next logical step is to set the scope for our security assessment. While doing assessments, sometimes we need to go through white-listed IP addresses using upstream proxies with Burp. We will cover that in the next chapter.

3
Setting the Scope and Dealing with Upstream Proxies

In the preceding chapter, we saw how to set up Mozilla Firefox with the FoxyProxy Standard add-on to create a selective, pattern-based forwarding process. This allows us to ensure that only white-listed traffic from our browser reaches Burp. This is something that Burp allows us to set with its configuration options itself. Think of it like this: less traffic reaching Burp ensures that Burp is dealing with legitimate traffic, and its filters are working on ensuring that we remain within our scope.

As a security professional testing web application, *scope* is a term you hear and read about everywhere. Many times, we are expected to test only parts of an application, and usually, the scope is limited by domain, subdomain, folder name, and even certain filenames. Burp gives a nice, simple-to-use interface to add, edit, and remove targets from the scope.

Multiple ways to add targets to the scope

Burp has a subtab called **Scope** under the **Target** tab. The most common way to add a target to Scope is to navigate to it using your browser, find it in the **Site map** subtab under the **Target** tab, right-click on it, and select **Add to scope**.

For example, if we have permission to test `http://download.mozilla.org`, and we want to add it to the scope, we do the following:

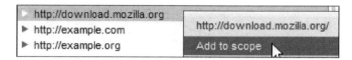

We can always edit the URL in the URL editor window if we need to tweak it a bit or if we made any mistakes and added something we shouldn't add. Have a look at the following screenshot:

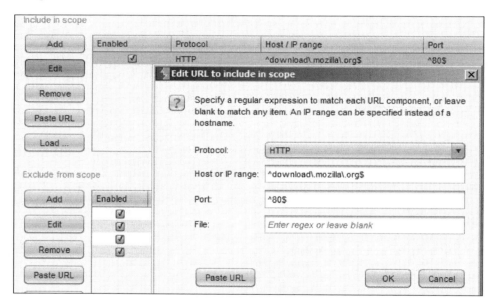

Apart from adding the URL to the scope using the context menu, we can always paste the URL of the target as well. When we paste the URL, we can choose the protocol, host/IP, port, and filename.

Loading a list of targets from a file

Loading a list of targets from a file is the most sensible way of adding targets to the scope in Burp. In most security assessment scenarios, we are already aware of exact URLs for our targets. This allows us to build a target list, which can simply be loaded into the **Scope** section by clicking on the **Load ...** button. Have a look at the following screenshot:

Once clicked, the **File Browser** dialog window opens and we can choose our file. The links need to be one of each line and based on their protocol, port number, path, and so on. All the fields get set up automatically. The following screenshot contains a list of sample target URLs for illustration. Note that some of the URLs in the following screenshot may not exist in reality:

```
http://example.com
http://www.example.com
http://example.org
http://www.example.org
https://www.example.com
http://example.com:8080
http://www.example.com/admin/file-upload
```

Scope and Burp Suite tools

Almost all the tools follow the scope. Most of the tools might offer more granular options over and above the Suite's scope. From Burp's application documentation, the following are the advantages of these tools:

- You can set display filters for the target site map and Proxy HTTP history. This allows us to focus on the task at hand, and everything else is kept hidden away.
- The Proxy can be configured to only intercept in-scope items — a highly desirable option in my opinion.
- Only in-scope items for spidering or live scanning in the scanner can be done.

Since most of the time, the activities that we carry out are undistinguishable from regular web attacks, it is extremely important to only attack targets that we want to without any shred of doubt. The target scope allows us to be precise just like that.

Scope inclusion versus exclusion

The target scope works on URL patterns. URL patterns can either be inclusive or exclusive. An inclusive pattern will allow all URLs matching the pattern to go through. An exclusive pattern will disallow all URLs matching the pattern from proceeding further. To match the scope, Burp Suite matches URLs to the patterns defined in the included list first. This allows us to add targets easily in scope. Once a target URL pattern is matched, it is checked against in the exclusion list. This is done to ensure that we don't inadvertently trigger critical functionality. For example, if we want to attack everything and not get logged out, we can exclude the **Logout** page. If some functionality triggers automated e-mails to thousands of users, we don't want to annoy the users by sending e-mails while testing by mistake. We should explicitly put the mentioned URLs in the exclusion list.

Spending some quality time figuring out the scope, adding the required target URLs, and ensuring that our inclusion and exclusion lists will ensure, will save us a lot of time and effort while using the other tools of the Suite. This might also be mandatory based on the testing activity we are planning to do. I highly recommend you to get comfortable using **Target Scope**.

Dropping out-of-scope requests

In the **Options** subtab under the **Connections** tab, we can decide how we would like to treat requests that are out of scope. Out-of-scope requests are any requests that don't match the URL patterns set in the **Scope** subtab.

A good plan is to drop all out-of-scope requests when you are absolutely sure about what you are attacking. You might want to reconsider based on requirements, especially if you are still figuring out the complete scope or functionality of the application being tested. Take a look at the following screenshot:

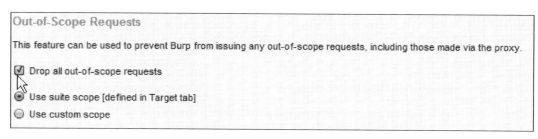

Dealing with upstream proxies and SOCKS proxies

Sometimes, the application that we need to test lies inside some corporate network. The clients give access to a specific IP address that is white-listed in the corporate firewall. At other times, we work inside the client location but it requires us to provide an internal proxy to get access to the staging site for testing.

In all such cases and more, we need to be able to add an additional proxy that Burp can send data to before it reaches our target. In some cases, this proxy can be the one that the browser requires to reach the intranet or even the Internet. Since we would like to intercept all the browser traffic and Burp has become the proxy for the browser, we need to be able to chain the proxy to set the same in Burp.

Types of proxies supported by Burp

We can configure additional proxies by navigating to **Options** | **Connections**.

If you notice carefully, the upstream proxy rule editor looks like the FoxyProxy add-on proxy window. That is not surprising as both of them operate with URL patterns. We can carefully add the target as the destination that will require a proxy to reach to.

Most standard proxies that support authentication are supported in Burp. Out of these, NTLM flavors are regularly found in networks with the Microsoft Active Directory infrastructure. The usage is straightforward. Add the destination and the other details that should be provided to you by the network administrators.

Working with SOCKS proxies

SOCKS proxies are another common form of proxies in use. The most popular SOCKS-based proxy is TOR, which allows your entire browser traffic, including DNS lookups, to occur at the proxy end. Since the SOCKS proxy protocol works by taking all the traffic through it, the destination server can see the IP address of the SOCKS proxy.

You can give this a whirl by running the Tor browser bundle `http://www.torproject.org/projects/torbrowser.html.en`. Once the Tor browser bundle is running successfully, just add the following values in the SOCKS proxy settings of Burp. Make sure you check **Use SOCKS proxy** after adding the correct values. Have a look at the following screenshot:

Using SSH tunneling as a SOCKS proxy

Using SSH tunneling as a SOCKS proxy is quite useful when we want to give a white-listed IP address to a firewall administrator to access an application. So, the scenario here requires you to have access to a GNU/Linux server with a static IP address, which you can connect to using **Secure Shell Server (SSH)**.

In Mac OS X and GNU/Linux shell, the following command will start a local SOCKS proxy:

```
ssh -D 12345 user@hostname.com
```

Once you are successfully logged in to your server, leave it on so that Burp can keep using it. Now add `localhost` as **SOCKS proxy host** and `12345` as **SOCKS proxy port**, and you are good to go.

In Windows, if we use a command-line SSH client that comes with GNU, the process remains the same. Otherwise, if you are a PuTTY fan, let's see how we can configure the same thing in it.

In PuTTY, follow these steps to get the SSH tunnel working, which will be our SOCKS proxy:

1. Start PuTTY and click on **SSH** and then on **Tunnels**.
2. Here, add a newly forwarded port. Give it the value of `12345`. Under **Destination**, there is a bunch of radio buttons; choose **Auto** and **Dynamic**, and then click on the **Add** button:

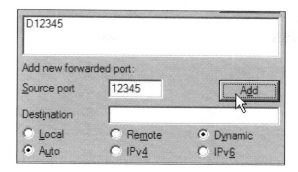

3. Once this is set, connect to the server.

4. Add the values `localhost` and `12345` in the **Host** and **Port** fields, respectively, in the Burp options for the SOCKS proxy.

5. You can verify that your traffic is going through the SOCKS proxy by visiting any site that gives you your external IP address. I personally use my own web page for that `http://akashm.com/ip.php`; you might want to try `http://icanhazip.com` or `http://whatismyip.com`.

Burp allows maximum connectivity with upstream and SOCKS proxies to make our job easier. By adding URL patterns, we can choose which proxy is connected in upstream proxy providers. SOCKS proxies, due to their nature, take all the traffic and send it to another computer, so we can't choose which URL to use it for. But this allows a simple-to-use workflow to test applications, which are behind corporate firewalls and need to white-list our static IP before allowing access.

Setting up Burp to be a proxy server for other devices

So far, we have run Burp on our computer. This is good enough when we want to intercept the traffic of browsers running on our computer. But what if we would like to intercept traffic from our television, from our iOS, or Android devices? Currently, in the default configuration, Burp has started one listener on an internal interface on port number `8080`. We can start multiple listeners on different ports and interfaces.

We can do this in the **Options** subtab under the **Proxy** tab. Note that this is different from the main **Options** tab. We can add more than one proxy listener at the same time by following these steps:

1. Click on the **Add** button under **Proxy Listeners**.

2. Enter a port number. It can be the same 8080, but if it confuses you, can give the number 8081.

3. Specify an interface and choose your LAN IP address.

4. Once you click on **Ok**, click on **Running**, and now you have started an external listener for Burp:

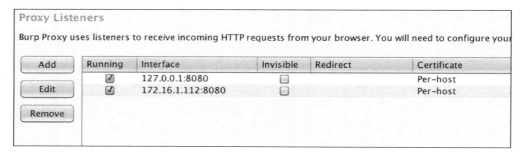

You can add the LAN IP address and the port number you added as the proxy server on your mobile device, and all HTTP traffic will get intercepted by Burp. Have a look at the following screenshot:

Summary

Now you know how to restrict the scope of HTTP traffic you would like to intercept. You saw how to include and exclude URL patterns for targets to configure, what in-scope is, and what out-of-scope is. Additionally, you learned how to configure Burp to be able to talk to other proxy servers if required and how to use the SOCKS proxy server, especially in a SSH tunnel kind of scenario.

You also learned how simple it is to create multiple listeners for Burp, which allows other devices in the network to send their HTTP traffic to the Burp interception proxy. The next chapter covers how to configure a proxy for SSL and other advanced settings that can be configured with Burp Suite.

4
SSL and Other Advanced Settings

Until now, we have successfully managed to intercept HTTP traffic. This is incredibly useful for a security professional tasked with the testing of applications that talk about HTTP. However, in our experience. we know that most secure applications are not served over HTTP, which is plain text, but over HTTP over **Secure Socket Layer (SSL)**.

HTTPS is a combination of HTTP over SSL/TLS to prevent eavesdropping, tampering, and MITM attacks.

To intercept traffic over HTTPS, we need to configure some more settings.

Browsers and servers exchange X.509 certificates, which are signed by certificate authorities. Since Burp runs at a layer below the layer in which encryption takes place, the content of the web page is already encrypted when it reaches Burp.

The only way Burp can see the data is if the SSL/TLS connection terminates here. So, Burp generates a per-site certificate, which the browser needs to accept. Since this certificate is not signed by a certificate authority known to us, we encounter an invalid certificate error, as shown in the following screenshot:

This Connection is Untrusted

You have asked Firefox to connect securely to **www.mozilla.org**, but we can't confirm that your connection is secure.

Normally, when you try to connect securely, sites will present trusted identification to prove that you are going to the right place. However, this site's identity can't be verified.

What Should I Do?

If you usually connect to this site without problems, this error could mean that someone is trying to impersonate the site, and you shouldn't continue.

Get me out of here!

▶ **Technical Details**

▶ **I Understand the Risks**

At this point, we can accept the error and interception will work exactly how we expect it to work. A more elegant approach is to import the Burp Suite root certificate into the browser we use for our testing. This way, we will get per-site unique certificates, and also, there will be no more errors about wrong/untrustworthy certificates.

Importing the Burp certificate in Mozilla Firefox

Starting with Mozilla Firefox, it is quite simple to import the certificate:

1. While Burp is running, go to `http://burp`.
2. Click on **CA Certificate**. Note where this file is downloaded:

The method is very convenient for testers, but it does open the tester to a malicious user who could perform MITM attacks against the pentester, abusing the trust related to the Burp Suite root certificate.

3. Open Firefox **Options**, click on **Advanced, Certificates**, and **View Certificates**. Have a look at the following screenshot:

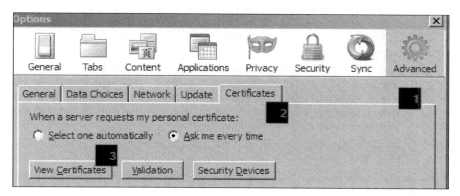

4. Click on **Authorities**, click on the **Import** button, and navigate to the place where you downloaded the certificate, as shown in the following screenshot:

5. You will get another window about whether you trust the new certificate authority. Select **Trust this CA to identify web sites**. And if you like, click on **View** to examine the CA certificate:

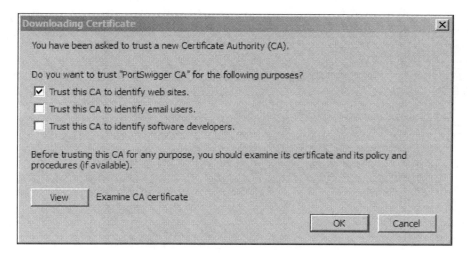

6. Click on the **OK** button and then navigate to `https://burp`. If there are no errors or warnings about the certificate, you installed it successfully.

Importing the Burp certificate in Microsoft IE and Google Chrome

Google Chrome uses the same certificate store as Microsoft Internet Explorer. Adding the certificate from either one of them is enough for us. Since IE is almost always installed by default, let's install the certificate in that first:

1. Open Internet Explorer options, and click on the **Content** tab, as shown in the following screenshot:

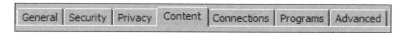

2. Internet Explorer provides us with a simple **Certificate Import Wizard**. Do note that the extension for the certificate is `.der`, which might not be visible in the file-browse dialog. Just select all files and you will be able to see them:

3. Accept the security warning about adding a root CA, and we are good to go, as shown in the following screenshot:

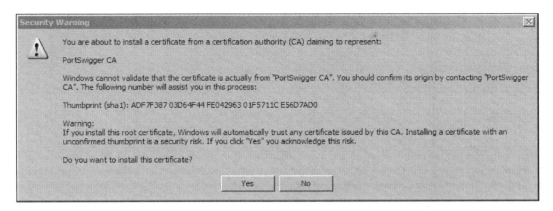

4. Navigate to `https://burp` to confirm that the certificate is installed correctly and working fine.

Installing the Burp certificate in iOS or Android

The basic steps remain the same. We need to figure out where the certificate should get installed. For iOS, since there is no simple way to add external files, Burp documentation suggests e-mailing the certificate file to yourself and saving it from there.

As long as we have proper privileges, we can install the root certificate on our devices.

SSL pass-through

Sometimes due to the way applications and websites are set up, it may not be possible to intercept SSL traffic. Usually, Burp will show an SSL negotiation error in the **Alerts** tab. One of the most common cases is when a mobile application utilizes certificate pinning. In such a scenario, when we still want to keep working with the other parts of the application, we can add the host in the SSL pass-through list.

This can be automated by checking an option, which will kick in as soon as Burp encounters an SSL negotiation error. Have a look at the following screenshot:

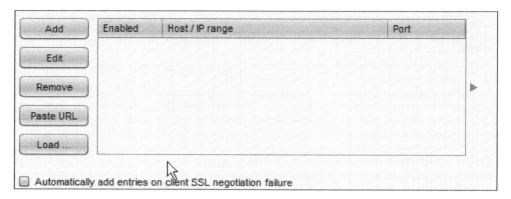

Invisible Proxy

Sometimes, while intercepting a thick client, you might need to enable **Invisible Proxy**. A thick client is a software that usually runs outside of the browser framework. This means that some of this software doesn't have an option for HTTP proxies. When the client is not proxy-aware and is incapable of sending requests that are used by a proxy, such as Burp, we need to use the option of **Invisible Proxy**.

Since a thick client has no proxy options, we need to trick it into sending all its traffic to the machine where the Burp proxy can listen. For example, if the nonproxy-aware thick client needed to connect to `https://example.com`, this is what we need to do:

1. Add a mapping for a domain to the loopback IP address in the default `Hosts` file. This file is usually found in the following paths for Windows and Linux / OS X:

    °   `Windows/System32/drivers/etc/hosts`

    °   `/etc/hosts`

    The mapping will look like this:

    `127.0.0.1  example.com`

2. Once this is set, we need to add a new listener running on the default port for HTTP TCP port number 80 or, if the traffic was meant to be over HTTPS, then TCP port number 443. Most likely, you need to be a privileged user on the system to be able to listen on those two ports, as shown in the following screenshot:

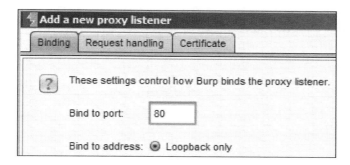

3. If the expected traffic is going to be over SSL, we need to ensure that we can present an SSL certificate to the thick client with an accurate domain name, as shown in the following screenshot:

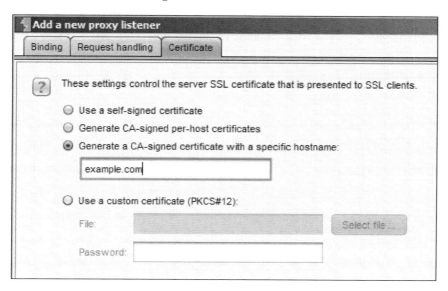

4. Now, we need to send the traffic from Burp to the original server, which is expecting it. We set this in **Options | Connections | Hostname Resolution**. We can't miss this step because we told the operating system to send all the traffic meant for `example.com` to the loopback interface earlier. Have a look at the following screenshot:

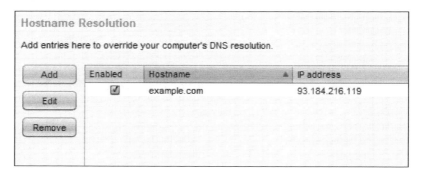

5. At this point, we have tricked the thick client (the nonproxy-aware application) to send all the traffic meant for `example.com` to the Burp Suite listener, and if required, present a correct SSL certificate as well. Once the traffic reaches Burp Suite, it can send it on its way to `example.com`.

6. There is a small caveat in all of this. Burp Suite uses the `Host` header in the request to figure out where to send the request further. If the `Host` header is not present in the request (rare, but can happen), we can configure Burp Suite to send all the traffic reaching a particular listener on to another server.

7. If the traffic is meant for multiple servers and we need to see all of it, then the only suggested solution is to create additional virtual interfaces where we can start loopback listeners, and if that is not an option, start Burp Suite on multiple computers to do what we did.

Summary

After this chapter, we can intercept SSL-enabled traffic for any website. While using SSL/TLS certificates is desirable in terms of security, it does pose a challenge when we wish to use an interception proxy, such as Burp, to test the website for flaws.

Burp provides a simple interface to set up SSL/TLS connections with minimal fuss. Once a root certificate authority is imported, all certificates generated by Burp and signed by the same root CA are identified as valid in the browsers. With this configuration, we have basically covered all that we needed to move on to learning about the various tools of Burp Suite that make it such a powerful tool to security test applications that work over HTTP.

5
Using Burp Tools As a Power User – Part 1

Burp Suite is powerful due to its amazing set of tools. In this chapter, we will look at some of these. We will start with Target, covering Site map and Scope, and move to Proxy, which is the work horse for testers. Then, we move on to the attack tool of choice, Intruder. No matter how much we talk about Intruder, it will not be enough, as this versatile tool can be used in a multitude of ways and combinations. After Intruder, we cover the Scanner tool and discuss when it is a good time to use the Scanner tool. We end the chapter with the Repeater tool, which supercharges the manual testing part by making it dead simple to repeat requests and see responses.

Most of us get started using the Proxy tool of Burp. The fact that Burp always starts with the **Intercept** mode switched on means that for everyone, the **Proxy** tab is the first thing they will see and use in the Burp interface. Other tools in Burp Suite, such as the Target, Proxy, Intruder, Scanner, and Repeater, are powerful as well. Their real power comes when these powerful tools are combined together to get the job done.

This and the next chapter are all about understanding these powerful tools individually and then learning to combine them for maximum impact.

Target

While Proxy remains the main tool, the **Target** tab is like our desktop. We assemble all our tools, files, and folders before embarking on a major project. The **Target** tab allows us to do just that. The **Target** tab has two subtabs for **Scope** and **Site map**. The **Scope** subtab allows us to set the scope for our testing (already covered in the previous chapters) and the **Site map** subtab shows us all requested and unrequested items for the website. The **Site map** subtab automatically collects data from other sources, including Proxy, Spider, active and passive Scanner (if configured), and content discovery.

The following screenshot shows how **Site map** creates a visual map that aids us in our understanding of the layout of the web application:

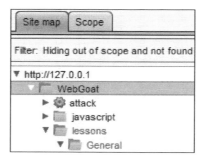

What are the advantages of having the entire site as a map in one place? There are many. To begin with, it provides a nice visual indication about whether we are on track with our scope or not. A site map using visual cues can indicate which web pages or links have already been visited and which haven't. This is indicated by showing the unrequested items in gray color. Ideally, you want to browse all the unrequested items. Sort all the items based on the **Time requested** column to see all unrequested items. The requested items show up in a darker color as opposed to the unrequested items, as shown in the following screenshot:

The ability to see the entire web application mapped out is incredibly powerful. Burp makes it more powerful by ensuring that regardless of how data about the website is gathered, it is updated in **Site map**. Therefore, any data gathered using passive or active scanning, spidering, or any other technique also gets updated here.

A site map allows testers to understand the application's structure and the design patterns with one look. It tells us which frameworks, technologies, and plugins are being used and whether there are any resources that might tell us more about the website.

Just as with any data aggregation tool, more power comes when we select data on various parameters, and Burp's **Display** filters do a great job here.

If you have added the scope properly, I recommend that you show only in-scope items and focus on working with those site maps. Based on the kind of application being tested, filter by MIME type, or status code, or just search for a specific string:

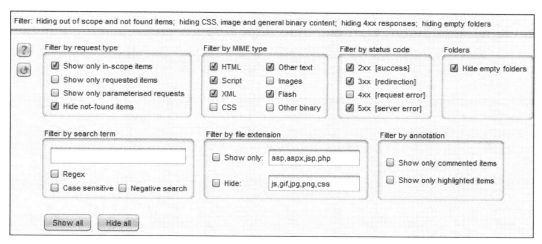

While mapping the application, it might make sense to uncheck **Hide not-found items**. This might point to some resource that was present earlier and give hints about the application and its flaws.

Now is a good time to look at the table view, and highlight and annotate the items that interest you. A login request is a good candidate to test for SQL injection later.

Highlight and annotate any request that you might want to look at again. Just right-click on a request, choose **Highlight** from the context menu, or double-click on the **host** column for any row to do the same thing. Similarly, you can add a comment by choosing **Add Comment** from the context menu, or by double-clicking on the **Comment** column and adding your comment.

We can filter highlighted and annotated information using the available display filters. I personally find commented items more useful to remember my thoughts and highlighted items to quickly sort the kind of testing I plan to do on requested items:

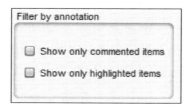

Site map compare

A great use case for a site map is when we want to know if there is any difference in the requests made by two uses with the same privileges or between uses at different privilege levels. For example, an application I tested requested all the endpoints while a user tried to log in. Based on the user privilege, there will be responses with different HTTP status codes. A comparison between the site map of a regular user and an admin user revealed more than 10 differences. For a tester, such information can be invaluable. A great tip from the Burp Suite documentation is to first map the entire application as a high-privileged user and then as a low-privileged user. The comparison will clearly show any access control violations that might be present.

To compare site maps, right-click on the domain in the **Target** tab, and choose **Compare site maps**:

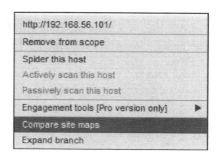

The basic flow for this functionality goes like this:

1. Once the **Compare site maps** option is selected, we choose the source for site maps. One source can be the current site map, and another can be loaded from a saved session. Have a look at the following screenshot:

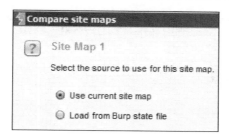

2. Burp can perform a comparison of the first and the second site maps by comparing the requests sent based on the URL file path, HTTP method, URL query string, and so on.

3. The responses can also be compared for response team headers, form field values, and so on.

4. Use the display filters to understand what the exact differences between the two site maps are.

The site map comparison is a good example of the differences between an automated tool, which most likely generates false positives, and Burp Suite, which forces you to think about privilege separation, but at the same time, it ensures that you can manually compare the two.

Proxy

While Burp Suite is a lot more than just a proxy, everything starts with configuring browsers to proxy through Burp. We covered the configuration of proxies extensively in the earlier chapters.

Using Proxy is an integral part of what Burp calls the **user-driven workflow**. The idea is that Burp sits in the middle of your HTTP client (mostly a browser) and the web server. Have a look at the following diagram:

There are primarily two ways of using Proxy. One is when the interception is turned off and the other when the interception is turned on. Take a look at the following screenshot:

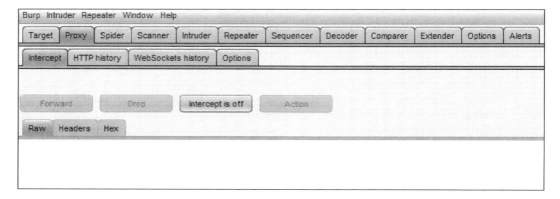

Proxy and, to some extent, Target tools are mainly meant for reconnaissance, mapping, and analysis of the web application being tested.

This doesn't seem as exciting as finding and exploiting vulnerabilities, but as most experienced testers realize with the passage of time, getting this phase correct is extremely important, if not compulsory. When the intercept is off, we are busy interacting with the application in our browser, and the Target site map is quietly building all the links and mapping them for us. When intercept is on, we switch between the browser window and the Burp Proxy **Intercept** tab to be able to view or edit the request, perform actions, such as sending it forward to the server or dropping the request. We can also choose to send the request to Scanner, Intruder, or Repeater for further processing.

 The process for dealing with websites with HTTPS is the same once we have configured the Burp SSL certificate properly in our browser (*Chapter 4, SSL and Other Advanced Settings*).

When you work in the intercept mode, you need to constantly switch between the browser window and Burp Suite. It pays to learn the keyboard shortcuts to switch windows in your operating system and also some of the keyboard shortcuts in use to work with the intercept mode.

Once you have fired a request in the browser, switch to Burp Suite using *Alt + Tab* in Windows and Ubuntu and *Cmd + Tab* in Mac. Whenever there is a request waiting for you in the **Intercept** tab, the taskbar will flash Burp Suite. Inside Burp, type in *Ctrl + Shift + P* to easily switch to the **Proxy** tab and *Ctrl + F* to forward the waiting request.

To see all the keyboard shortcuts or edit them,
go to **Options** | **Misc** | **HotKeys**.

The Message Analysis tab

Burp's most amazing feature is the fact that it doesn't hide away the raw HTTP
packets behind the pretty GUI. The **Message Analysis** tab gives you multiple
ways to look at and deal with the intercepted requests. The default view is **Raw**.
Have a look at the following screenshot:

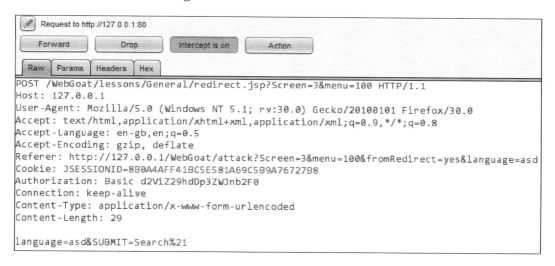

The subtabs that can be present include **XML**, **AMF**, and **View State**; these are
only available when the request and response are of that type. Have a look at the
following subtabs:

- **Raw**: This subtab is a text editor; requests can be changed from here.

- **Params**: This subtab is useful for easy viewing of parameters for HTTP
  requests. We can edit it by double-clicking on the column.

- **Headers**: Just like **Params**, name-value pairs are shown in a tabular form.
  This can be edited by double-clicking on the name-value pairs.

- **Hex**: This gives data in hex format with a hex editor built-in. Individual bytes
  can be edited by providing hex values.

- **HTML**: If the HTTP response contains HTML in the message body, the **HTML**
  tab can be used.

- **XML**: If the HTTP response contains XML in the message body, the **XML** tab can be used.

- **Render**: If you want to see the rendered HTML page in Burp itself, this option is useful.

- **View State**: This is used to obtain an unencrypted view state for the ASP. NET platform. The contents are shown in a tree format and in a raw format. We can edit the raw format, and the tree will be redrawn. This is only useful if the server-side ASP.NET is not MAC-enabled.

- **AMF**: This tab shows **Action Message Format** used by Flash. The contents are displayed in a tree structure, allowing editing of data values.

We can easily modify the display settings for the **Message Analysis** tab:

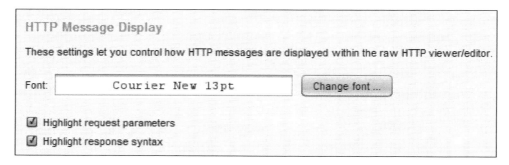

Actions on the intercepted requests

Once we have an intercepted request, we can send it to Repeater (*Ctrl + R*) to manipulate it one by one; we can send it to Intruder (*Ctrl + I*) to simulate an automated attack; we can send it for more spidering, an active scan or even to a Sequencer, Decoder, or Comparer (covered in the next chapter):

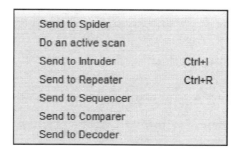

The question to ask is what should decide whether we should use Repeater or Intruder?. The short answer is, it is up to you. I personally use Repeater to figure out whether there is a flaw worth using Intruder or not. An active scan is always the last resort for the sake of completeness. This might change based on time and scope as well.

Repeater is like REPL for application security testing. Just like Read-Eval-Print-Loop is an interactive environment to try out any programming language, it allows a tester to send requests and get instant feedback with the responses.

Intruder is like an iterator. We give it a range of values and unleash it on the application. In most cases, the output of basic test cases from Repeater will point you either to use Intruder or go with the active scanner.

Logical issues and input-based issues are better tested and verified with Repeater once and then exploited using Intruder.

We will spend more time looking at engagement tools in *Chapter 8, Using Engagement Tools and Other Utilities,* so let's talk about adding the intercept requests to Scope. From the context menu, we can easily modify the scope and ensure that we can exclude the intercept requests based on the host, IP address, file extension, and directory. Take a look at the following screenshot:

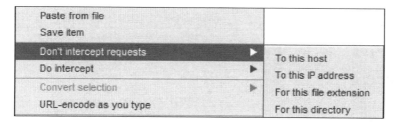

Requesting in the browser allows us to do two things:

- The original request uses the same session cookie as the request in the browser.

- The request is reissued with the session's cookie information from the browser. This can be useful to test access control, where requests generated by one user (in Burp) can be compared to another user, such as an administrator (in the browser).

Response interception and modification

By default, Burp doesn't intercept responses. You can easily intercept a response for an intercepted request by choosing that in the context menu. If you would like to intercept all responses, the same can be configured in **Proxy Options** accordingly.

To intercept responses, we need to perform the following steps:

1. Check the **Intercept responses based on the following rules:**, as shown in the screenshot that appears after the next point in this series of steps.

2. We can choose when to intercept a response:
   - Ideally only intercept if the request is modified
   - A request is intercepted
   - The request is in scope

   This is shown in the following screenshot:

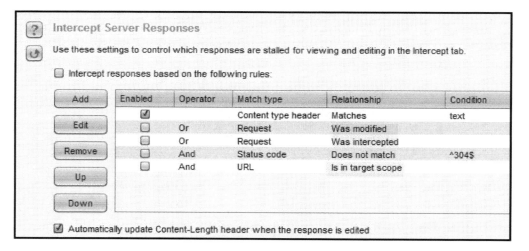

3. Apart from interceptions, we can also automodify responses based on rules and what we would like to choose, as shown in the following screenshot:

Response Modification

These settings are used to perform automatic modification of responses.

- [ ] Unhide hidden form fields
    - [ ] Prominently highlight unhidden fields
- [ ] Enable disabled form fields
- [ ] Remove input field length limits
- [ ] Remove JavaScript form validation
- [ ] Remove all JavaScript
- [ ] Remove <object> tags
- [ ] Convert HTTPS links to HTTP
- [ ] Remove secure flag from cookies

Using the Proxy history tab

The Proxy history, in my opinion, is the single most important data store for any security testing project. Burp maintains all of it in the **HTTP history** subtab. The **History** table has a lot of columns to manage, analyze, and work with the data. All the columns are sortable by clicking on their headings. In a lot of security assessments, allowing the site map to fill up and then going through the **HTTP history** table gives us a very good idea about the functionality, architecture, and common patterns that might indicate vulnerabilities and more.

The **History table** subtab has many columns providing useful information.

You can read more about the columns in the online Burp Suite documentation under the **History table** heading:

`http://portswigger.net/burp/help/proxy_history.html`

Have a look at the following screenshot:

Out of the columns in this screenshot, one should pay close attention to the **Params** column, which indicates that we have parameters that can be fuzzed using Intruder and status, which tells us what kind of responses we are getting. For example, when a user is able to log in successfully to WordPress, they get a HTTP status code **302** as opposed to status code **200** for an unsuccessful login. A good tester will also try to fuzz the HTTP method (under the **Method** column) for sensitive requests, using Repeater.

If we use display filters, it is quite possible that some of the requests will seem missing. They are just hidden due to the filters. Ideally, we want to look at only in-scope requests and ignore images and **Cascading Style Sheet** (**CSS**) files to begin with. Similar to the site map table, we can annotate and highlight requests that might be useful for later. It is useful to sort out whether a request/response was modified by the user, which indicates all requests that have parameters we can fuzz and were edited before being sent to the server as part of our interception.

Unlike the **Message Analysis** window under the **Intercept** tab, we can't edit the **Message Analysis** window under **HTTP history**. This makes sense, as this is a historical record of every request and response made to the application while Burp was configured as a proxy. We can use the menu having a similar context to figure out our next move in terms of sending a request for further discovery or exploitation of vulnerability or save the request response in a text file as well.

Intruder

Burp Intruder is meant for exploitation and automating attacks. Most of the attacks against web applications are about sending them a lot of data and making sense of the responses. Therefore, Intruder is a very good and efficient request sender and response collector. The tool is incredibly flexible and infinitely customizable. That is great once you have the hang of it, but can be a bit overwhelming for someone just starting out.

The best way to get started is to find a request that has parameters that can be fuzzed. A login form is a good example where we can check for weak credentials by simulating a dictionary attack using the Intruder tool.

First, we choose an interesting-looking request that can and should be automated. A few examples of this would be:

- Enumerating user information, such as names and passwords
- Enumerating common directories and files that can cause information leakage
- Fuzzing for XSS, SQLI, and path traversals

Basically, we give a baseline request to Intruder, mark the positions where the payloads or attack test cases should be placed, and start the attack. The Pro version of Burp comes with a lot of attack payloads, but it is a good idea to add to the collection by getting more payloads from:

- FuzzDB
- Web App URLs (`https://github.com/pwnwiki/webappurls`)
- The OWASP DirBuster Project

Once we have enough payloads, we just need to set the positions, and we are good to go. The shortcut for this is to go to the **HTTP history** table and pick up a request that has parameters and will nicely fit our automated attack scenario:

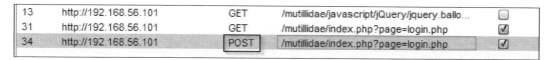

In the preceding screenshot, we can see that the same URL was requested using **GET** and then using **POST**. It is a login form and has parameters, so we can easily find positions for fuzzing. So, with a login form, we will try and guess the password using brute forcing.

Let's send this request to Intruder either using the context menu, as shown in the following screenshot, or using the keyboard shortcut *Ctrl + I*:

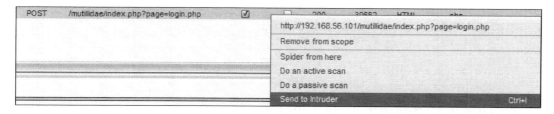

Now, getting to the attack part is a four-step process. Have a look at the following screenshot:

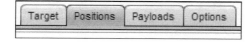

Here is how we attack:

1. First, it's about setting the target. This has already been set for us as we came from the Proxy tool. We can change the given values for **Host** and **Port** if required. Have a look at the following screenshot:

2. Then comes setting the positions. These are set using a position marker. Burp intelligently selects some positions for us, as shown in the following screenshot:

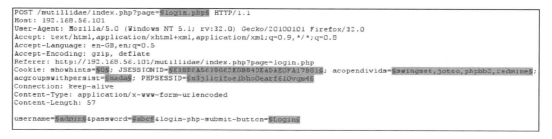

3. We might want to clear the default selection and just select the parameters we are interested in.

4. If the objective is to enumerate files and folders, the position for the path should be selected; here, we are trying to dictionary the password for the user admin. Therefore, we choose accordingly. We clear all the selections except the one surrounding the password field's value, as shown in the following screenshot:

```
POST /mutillidae/index.php?page=login.php HTTP/1.1
Host: 192.168.56.101
User-Agent: Mozilla/5.0 (Windows NT 5.1; rv:30.0) Gecko/20100101 Firefox/30.0
Accept: text/html,application/xhtml+xml,application/xml;q=0.9,*/*;q=0.8
Accept-Language: en-gb,en;q=0.5
Accept-Encoding: gzip, deflate
Referer: http://192.168.56.101/mutillidae/index.php?page=login.php
Cookie: showhints=0; PHPSESSID=n59d4uurbhujn0mkle36k152s4
Connection: keep-alive
Content-Type: application/x-www-form-urlencoded
Content-Length: 57

username=admin&password=§abc§&login-php-submit-button=Login
```

5. Now, we have the target and the position defined. It is time to choose the payloads. This is done on the **Payloads** tab. Each payload will replace the text present in the baseline request in the enclosed position markers that we have already defined. For our particular case, we will choose a simple list from the payload set. And then, we will add a list of passwords from the dropdown of **Add from list ...** from the list:

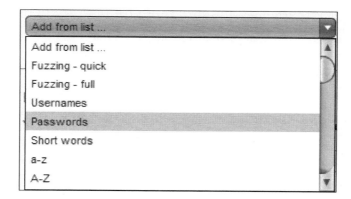

Apart from adding the payload set, we will also set a rule for payload processing. Payload processing adds programmability and unlimited customization for our payload set.

In our case, we are interested in fuzzing the password field and try our various passwords that can be possible for a given user.

If the following is the list of payloads, we have the following screenshot:

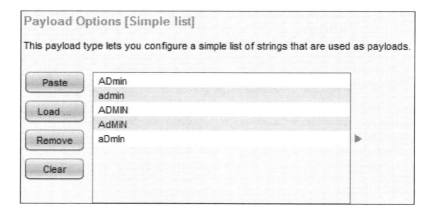

We can use **Payload Processing** to transform the payloads to suit our needs. Have a look at the following screenshot:

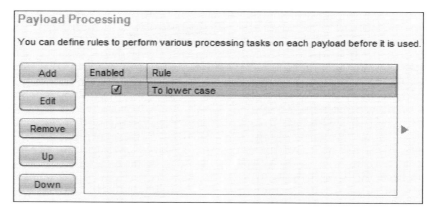

We can add the following types of rules to perform **Payload Processing**:

- Add prefix or suffix
- Match/replace
- Substring and reverse substring
- Modify case — to upper, lower, or sentence case
- Encode/decode — to URL, HTML, Base64, ASCII, JavaScript, and more
- Hash — from MD5 to up to SHA256
- Invoke another Burp Extension to do more than the given options

At this point, a lot of testers get confused and go to the next tab, which is to set all the options for Intruder.

What we need to do here is to go to **Intruder | Start Attack**. If you have thousands of payloads and multiple positions, it makes sense to save the attack configuration and then load it from the menu. If you want to add more payloads from other sources or maybe your internal test cases, you can do so using the **Configure predefined payload lists** option:

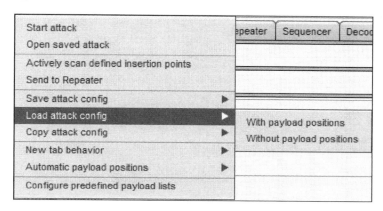

When we run Intruder, we run it with a certain configuration. While specifying the payload positions, we also have to specify the attack types. There are four defined, as follows:

- **Sniper**: Each payload is placed in the position one at a time
- **Battering Ram**: Each payload is placed in all the positions all at once
- **Pitchfork**: Multiple payloads for each position are placed
- **Cluster Bomb**: Multiple payloads for each position are placed, but all combinations of payloads and positions take place

The default attack type is a sniper. Based on the complexity of operation, you will need to choose the best option possible. Obviously, between **Sniper** and **Cluster Bomb**, the number of requests made due to the number of payloads and the number of positions is going to increase exponentially.

When that happens, we need to pay attention to the **Options** subtab in the **Intruder** tab, and do a **Grep – Match** action on responses. For our case, a logged in admin user can see **Logged In Admin** as text on the web page; therefore, we will see the following result after our dictionary attempt:

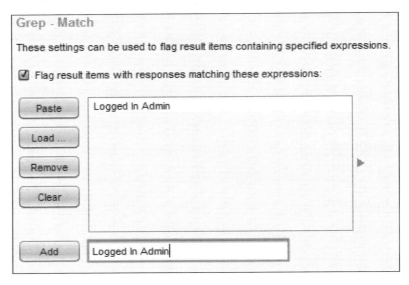

Grep is a powerful command-line tool from the *nix command line that provides us with an easy way to identify patterns.

The **Grep – Match** string, which in this case is **Logged In Admin**, becomes a column in the attack results table:

Request	Payload	Status	Error	Timeout	Length	Logged In Admin

In the attack results table, the fourteenth attack request was successful, and the column value for **Logged in Admin** is checked. This provides us with an easy way to identify when and where our attack succeeded, and the second column lists our payload as well:

| 13 | adIdemo | 200 | ☐ | ☐ | 39624 | ☐ |
| 14 | admin | 302 | ☐ | ☐ | 39785 | ☑ |

The Burp documentation on Intruder is unparalleled. The philosophy of a multipurpose, flexible, and infinitely customizable attack tool gives unprecedented control over crafting our attacks against web applications.

There are 18 payload types given in Burp. Some of the really interesting ones are:

- **Extension Generated**: We can use a specific type of Burp Extension to generate our payloads. As I said, this is infinitely customizable.

- **ECB Block Shuffler**: This is used to shuffle blocks of cipher text in ECB encrypted data to bypass application logic if required. Since ECB ciphers encrypt blocks independently, previously known plain text will give us predictable cipher text. There are attacks to manipulate this in application logic.

- **Character Frobber**: This is useful to check whether a unique value is being considered for processing or if changing one character has no effect on it.

- **Null Payloads**: Sometimes, we just want the application to generate and give us different values for every request that can be fed into the sequencer tool, which can be done using this option.

Other payload types include **Brute forcer, Character Blocks, Illegal Unicode**, and so on.

Intruder is very efficient at taking multiple test cases, and after processing (if required), it can quickly make the resultant requests and show the responses. Intruder, therefore, can be used to do username enumeration, test for insecure direct object reference issues, and forced browsing issues, and it is well suited for parameter fuzzing.

It is indeed an extremely powerful tool in the hands of an experienced web application security tester.

Scanner

Burp Scanner can automatically do vulnerability assessment of web applications.

We can conduct an active scan, which involves sending more data to the server, or passive scanning, which is basically looking for vulnerabilities passing through the **Proxy** tool. Either **Custom scope** can be set for the scanning, or active scanning can be done for the already existing suite scope.

The Burp Scanner tool can also be configured to provide a point-and-click scan, but this is not recommended according to the tool. Most web application scanners suffer from similar issues in terms of the following:

- The coverage of the application is one major issue. In most cases, automated scanners are unable to understand JavaScript or Flash content. In scanner terms, this is called **crawling**.

- If the crawling is not complete, all the functionality cannot be tested for security, and there is no clear way of saying whether the web application is secure or not.

- Most scanners are unable to manage the session handling part to test things, such as role-based access control, in an automatic fashion.

An active scan is a great idea when we have full control over what is being scanned. In the active scan mode, Burp sends different kinds of requests to the application and based on the response, verifies whether a particular kind of vulnerability exists or not.

The scanner options can be customized to understand what type of values will be fuzzed as part of the active scanning mode. Have a look at the following screenshot:

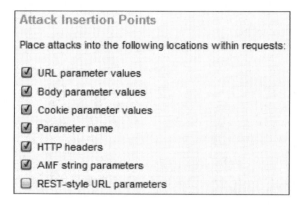

Based on the type of application being tested, these values should be changed.

An active scan can be triggered automatically. Take a look at the following screenshot:

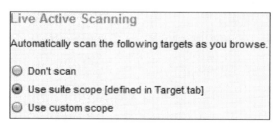

Sometimes, we need to initiate it manually from anywhere in the application using the context menu:

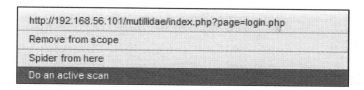

From the Burp documentation, the issues that Burp's active scanning is able to identify mostly fall into two categories:

- Input-based vulnerabilities targeting the client side, such as cross-site scripting, HTTP header injection, and open redirection
- Input-based vulnerabilities targeting the server side, such as SQL injection, OS command injection, and file path traversal

Scanning optimization and requests

There are important options on how performant the scanner should be while doing active scanning. A really fast scanner can unintentionally cause a denial of service on the application.

The other important thing to keep in mind is that if you want a more thorough scan, it will increase the number of requests sent to the server, due to which more work will need to be done by Burp to understand and translate the results for you.

A passive scan is the analysis of traffic passing through the proxy. Again, it makes sense to explicitly configure the scope so that the application doesn't have to do more work than necessary.

Burp Scanner is able to identify numerous kinds of vulnerabilities using solely passive techniques, including the ones mentioned at `http://portswigger.net/burp/help/scanner_scanmodes.html#passive`.

Some of the issues that are not very interesting to report, but are quite sensitive with respect to security, are:

- Clear-text submission of passwords
- Insecure cookie attributes, such as missing `HttpOnly`, and secure flags
- Caching of SSL-protected content
- Directory listings

When to scan

A sound strategy for a semi-automated web application penetration or vulnerability test involves understanding and deciphering the developer's mistakes. Usually, for an application developer, mistakes indicate patterns. These patterns reoccur in multiple places, and while we are doing manual testing of a particular module or section of the application, running an active scan for that particular section can quickly give us a good idea whether there are any low-lying vulnerabilities that get detected.

Some of the vulnerabilities that need to be detected and fixed are akin to rote work, which for a human, can become mundane very soon. Humans tend to make mistakes when they are tired or when not paying complete attention. At such times, the software can make our job easier by ensuring that we don't miss out reporting such issues for any nontechnical reasons.

Scan queues contain records of all the manual scanning that we initiated.

Repeater

Burp Repeater is a tool to send HTTP requests and see their responses one by one. Consider it like a scratch pad. You can manually change parameters, request methods, and see the response. The power of Repeater comes with its integration with the rest of the suite. We can send a request from anywhere to Repeater to be worked on, and we can create a brand new request as well:

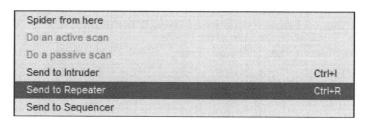

Repeater's user interface is quite bare, and it can seem a little confusing at first. As I mentioned before, the common way of using Repeater is to send a request to it. But otherwise, we need to set the **Host** and **Port** values we would like to send the request to. This can be done by clicking on the **Edit** host button in the top-right corner and adding the proper values. Have a look at the following screenshot:

Once the host and port are set, we can start making HTTP requests using a very basic interface, as shown in the following screenshot:

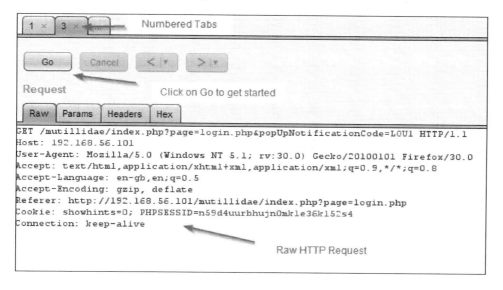

All the requests that get sent to the Repeater tool are sequentially numbered. If the request has been sent from **Proxy History** or from somewhere else, it will contain all the information coming from the browser, including any cookie values that have been set. This information is shown in an HTTP editor, and all other details about the request can be changed.

One of the most useful options we have is to change the request method for any HTTP request. This allows us to change a POST to a GET, and automatically all the parameters in the request body are converted into query string. The advantage of being able to make a GET request in lieu of a POST is to quickly pass that to any other tool that can accept and work with HTTP requests.

The best time to use Repeater is when using any other tool; you would like to investigate an interesting response for a request and see what could be happening. Sometimes, I use it to verify SQL injection or XSS or even to see if we can start extracting data from the attack on the server.

 A quick tip is to test any server acting as a mobile backend for the **OPTIONS** header and see what comes back.

Summary

After this chapter, we can use Proxy, Scanner, Target, Intruder, and Repeater. The important bit is to learn how to use these tools together. In a way, Burp Suite tools mimic how simple command-line utilities on a Unix/Linux command line can work together to fulfill complex tasks effectively. Similarly, Target, Proxy, Scanner, Intruder, and Repeater offer an infinite number of ways to interact and work with applications to test them for security.

Now, you should be aware of how and when to use which tool. The innate understanding on how they all fit comes from testing a variety of applications and facing challenges, which can be solved by combining the use of multiple tools together.

We are now prepared to talk more about the rest of the power tools in the Burp Suite arsenal.

6
Using Burp Tools As a Power User – Part 2

In the preceding chapter, we looked at the primary tools of Burp Suite, such as Proxy, Scanner, Target, Intruder, and Repeater. In this chapter, we will look at the other tools that make up the Burp Suite software and see how Spider, Sequencer, Decoder, Comparer, and Alerts work in sync to provide us with what we need to test web applications.

Spidering

Spidering or web crawling, as it is better known, is the process of automatically following all the links on a web page to discover both static and dynamic web resources of the web application. Burp uses the Spider tool to automate the mapping of an application.

The Burp documentation recommends that we complete our manual preparation and fill up the Target site map with what is currently visible to the browser and Burp Suite. Spidering, or crawling, of a website is a pretty intensive and performance-hungry activity. This is one of the main reasons that, before we plan to spider a production website, we should think really long and hard about any adverse effects on the performance of the website for its users while spidering is going on.

Along with the site performance, websites with rich content, such as Ajax and Adobe Flash-based content, may not get completely crawled as regular crawlers can't understand how to interact with such elements. So, parts of the functionality may not get detected if the spider encounters such elements on the web page.

Burp follows all the links that are in scope, tries out standard files and folders, and even submits forms with dummy data as part of its crawling and spidering activity. Ideally, we want to avoid polluting the production database with dummy data and be careful about which functionality to spider.

We can use the suite scope set in the **Target** tab for spidering and crawling. We can use a custom scope as well. The advantage of using the already-defined scope is obvious. Spider will try and complete the suite site map with links still not requested, and this will give us a better picture of the site being tested. Have a look at the following screenshot:

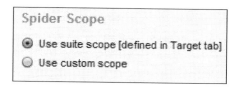

Sometimes, for a large website, we want to use spidering apart from passive scanning. It is prudent to set up **Crawler Settings** before any kind of spidering that you want to do. The default settings work in most cases but keep your use case in mind. All the options are selected by default:

Crawler Settings

These settings control the way the Spider crawls for basic web content.

☑ Check robots.txt
☑ Detect custom "not found" responses
☑ Ignore links to non-text content
☑ Request the root of all directories
☑ Make a non-parameterised request to each dynamic page

Maximum link depth: 5

Maximum parameterised requests per URL: 50

In a nonproduction environment, checking for `robots.txt` may not make a lot of sense. But many security professionals forget to check this file for pointers to understand how the website will be structured.

A website owner can inform any automatic crawler visiting their site about what is allowed to be crawled and what is not.

For example, for a staging website, which the website owner doesn't want crawled by Googlebot, they can add the following to `robots.txt`:

```
User-agent: *
Disallow: /
```

Most search engine bots will honor such a request and not crawl the website. On a production site, there might be sensitive directories that a website owner would rather not see in search results. For each of these directories, they can add a new line of text in the `robots.txt` file.

While this is great in terms of bots that will follow instructions, such a file gives valuable information to an attacker or a tester about what parts of the website are not being crawled.

Apart from following links and trying out common paths, Spider will also submit HTML forms. We can either set Spider to prompt us for each form that might need to be submitted, or we can set it to either not submit forms at all or completely automate form submission:

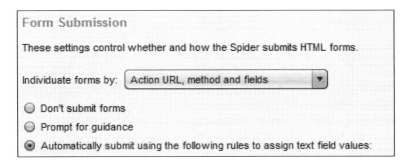

We can completely configure the form field values using either exact matches or regular expressions for the field names. For example, in the following screenshot, we have set regular expressions for a standard form field name, such as `mail` (this should match the e-mail), `first` (this should match the first name), and others. Do not forget to customize the values for these fields, as some of the forms might save data in a database. This way, if a production website has forms that get filled and submitted as part of an assessment, the client will be able to clearly see that it was part of our testing and not some random bot on the Internet.

We need to be careful about spidering dangerous functionality automatically. What if the admin dashboard had a link for `Delete all users` and just by clicking on it, we triggered it? A spider/crawler is meant to follow all links, and if that link is followed, we would end up deleting all the users. So, before we set up automatic spidering of content, especially in the case of features only available to authenticated users, we need to be careful about how to proceed:

Match type	Field name	Field value
Regex	mail	akashmahajan@gmail.com
Regex	first	Akash
Regex	last	Mahajan
Regex	surname	Mahajan
Regex	name	Akash Mahajan
Regex	comp	The App Sec Lab

As I mentioned before, spidering and crawling can be quite a drain on resources for the website. It is important to set up limits on the backend engine that powers Burp Spider to ensure that we don't inadvertently reduce the performance of the website. We can control this with the **Spider Engine** options. The most relevant option here is the **Number of threads** that we want to use for the crawling. Needless to say, more the number of threads, faster the crawling will be. Based on how much you want to crawl and how big the web application is, we might want to tinker with the following settings:

Spider Engine	
These settings control the engine used for making HTTP requests when spidering.	
Number of threads:	10
Number of retries on network failure:	3
Pause before retry (milliseconds):	2000
☐ Throttle between requests (milliseconds):	500
☐ Add random variations to throttle	

If you find frequent errors on the website, you might want to bring down the number of threads for the spidering engine. After all the options have been set, the scope has been determined, and the spider engine fine-tuned, all that remains to be done is start the spider. Once the spider has been started, we can toggle the same button to stop/pause the spidering. If required, we can even throw away all the scanning already done and start again:

Sequencer

Sequencer is an interesting tool that comes with Burp Suite. Sequencer allows us to test how random the data is.

Applications require different types of sufficiently random tokens for a multitude of things, for example, session IDs, anti-CSRF tokens, password reset tokens, user account activation tokens, and more. The basic question that we try to answer is that given enough number of tokens, will the randomness of the tokens be enough? Will a large enough sample of tokens reveal any patterns that allow us to guess a token value that might have been generated in the past or might occur in the future?

A good place to use the Sequencer tool is when you suspect that developers have tried to use their own code to create what they feel are random values, and that additionally those values are being used for some kind of authentication in the application. A simple enough example is to test the randomness of the cookie UID that is used for authentication by Mutillidae.

Mutillidae is a web application that was created to be deliberately insecure. It is a training application that we can use to learn more about OWASP top-10 risks faced by applications. We can learn how to attack such an application and what it will take to defend it. We can download it as a standalone application or with the OWASP Broken Web Applications live CD environment.

The steps to test for randomness of the tokens using Sequencer go like this:

1. Choose the exact value you would like to test. This can either be captured live by Burp generating the necessary traffic, or the already existing values can be passed to Burp.

2. In our example, we will send the response for the request that allowed generation of the UID cookie. Have a look at the following screenshot:

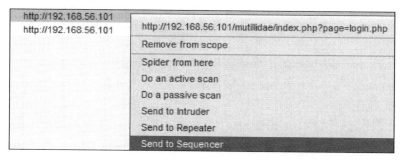

3. Burp has automatically selected cookies that might contain the value we would like to sequence. Take a look at the following screenshot:

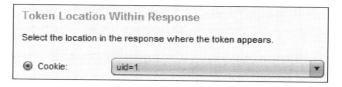

4. We can choose the default cookie values and even form fields when present or use the custom location dialog box. This dialog box is available to use when we choose custom locations and click on the **Configure** button. Have a look at the following screenshot:

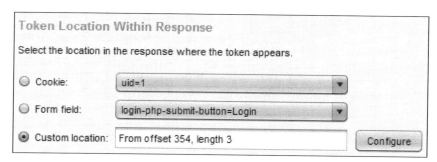

5. We can start by typing the text to begin the search for and the text to end the search with:

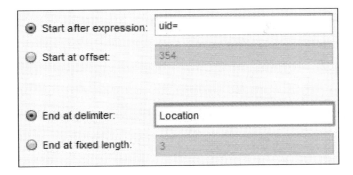

6. Alternatively, we can just work with an offset value and a fixed-length beginning from the offset. This does mean that we are closely familiar with the exact location of the value we are interested in extracting. Have a look at the following screenshot:

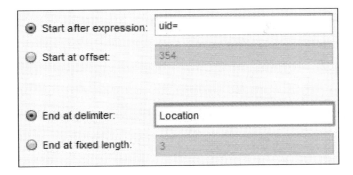

7. If we already have the tokens, we can click on the **Manual Load** tab and select them for Analysis. Have a look at the following screenshot:

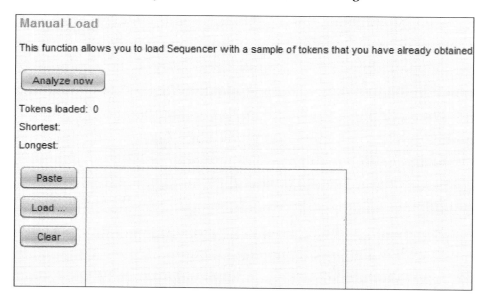

Analysis of the tokens

Adding the tokens is only the first part of using Sequencer. The analysis will tell us about the randomness and whether the token values are secure enough to be used for various kinds of authentication.

If the tokens require padding either at the beginning or the end or need to be Base64 encoded, we can choose that under **Token Handling**. Have a look at the following screenshot:

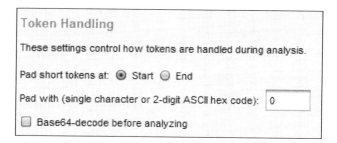

We can also choose what kind of analysis tests to perform. To begin with, it is recommended that you to leave all of them selected, and later when you have more understanding of the kind of token or the testing required, you can pick and choose, as shown in the following screenshot:

The randomness tests are based on statistical tests. The tests observe specific properties of the values being tested for randomness. Based on the observations, we get a probability of randomness. Each of the tests has a **significance level**. If the probability falls below this significance level, then the token is considered to be nonrandom.

There are primarily two ways to test the randomness: at the character level and at the bit level. You can read all about how the tests work in the excellent Burp Suite documentation at http://www.portswigger.net/burp/help/sequencer_tests.html.

Sample analysis

To get an idea of what kind of output Sequencer gives, we create two synthetic token loads.

First, using a simple command-line tool called **jot**, we generate 20,000 random numbers between 1 and 400000 manually loaded for analysis. Have a look at the following screenshot:

```
jot -r 20001 1 400000 | tee tokens-larger
```

Here is what we get as the output:

> Overall result
>
> The overall quality of randomness within the sample is estimated to be: extremely poor.
> At a significance level of 1%, the amount of effective entropy is estimated to be: 10 bits.

We repeated this with a load of 5000 UUIDs generated from the command line and loaded manually:

```
for i in `seq 1 5000`; do uuidgen | tee -a tokens-uuid; done
```

The output will be as follows:

> Overall result
>
> The overall quality of randomness within the sample is estimated to be: excellent.
> At a significance level of 1%, the amount of effective entropy is estimated to be: 99 bits.

For web application penetration testers, this is a useful result where we can compare the bits of entropy as a mathematical number and understand whether the randomness is poor or excellent. Sequencer is an excellent tool to do something quite challenging for most of us (unless we understand how to manually do all this analysis).

The analysis report with its overall result and graphs showcasing the different types of analysis done is incredibly useful.

Decoder

Decoder tool in Burp Suite does the job of encoding and decoding data. Applications need to encode data while transmitting it or, in many cases, as a security measure. Encoding is not a security measure but a lot of developers mistake it to be.

 A simple rule of thumb is that if there is no key present, there is no confidentiality. Since we don't require a key to encode a piece of plain text, we don't require a key to decode.

A web application penetration tester needs to be able to understand the type of encoding that has been applied and then successfully decode the piece of data.

As with all the other tools, we saw that:

- We can select a piece of text anywhere in Burp Suite and send it to Decoder. Have a look at the following screenshot:

- We can also do manual transforms (encoding or decoding) using the context menu wherever we are currently working, as shown in the following screenshot:

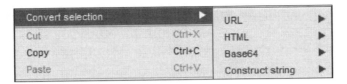

- We can do **URL-decode** and URL encode with different options using the context menu. Have a look at the following screenshot:

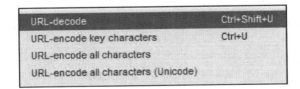

We can select the following piece of data:

```
page=user-info.php&username=%27+or+1%3D1&password=%27+or+1%3D1&us
er-info-php-submit-button=View+Account+Details&popUpNotificationCo
de=SUD1
```

This code can be transformed into the following:

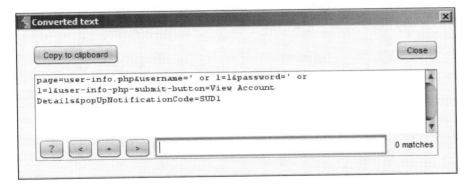

- Similarly, we can decode and encode HTML for all characters or key characters in numeric entities or hex entities, as shown in the following screenshot:

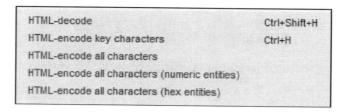

Often, we will encounter pieces of data that are vaguely familiar, but we aren't sure of the encoding used. We can use Smart Decode to recursively identify the hashing or encoding applied and decode the piece of data.

Comparer

Next in our tools for Burp Suite is Comparer. Comparer is simply a tool to compare to HTTP requests or responses.

Comparer is useful when you want to see how different values for parameters and headers enable subtle changes in the responses that you receive. It is useful to see how the application reacts to a valid user, invalid password combination compared to an invalid user and invalid password combination. This can aid in enumerating usernames.

Consider that a web application gives an informational error, such as a wrong password for a given username. All I need to do is supply different usernames, and for all those times, if I get the mentioned error, I will know for sure that those usernames exist in the web application.

Many times with Blind SQL injection, there can be tiny differences in HTTP responses, and the tool can help you identify exactly what is different.

We start by using the context menu to send either the HTTP request or response to the Comparer. have a look at the following screenshot:

Now, consider that we have two responses to compare. The first response is as follows:

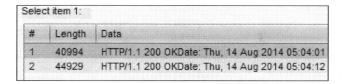

The second response is as follows:

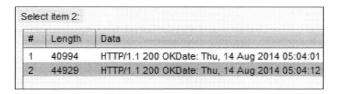

We can compare the responses using **Words** or **Bytes**. Byte-wise comparison is computationally very expensive, and the Burp documentation recommends that it should only be used when the **Words** comparison is not able to find the differences. Have a look at the following screenshot:

To make out the visual differences, it is useful to sync views while scrolling. When we sync the views, we can clearly make out what has changed between the two responses. We can visually see the differences in what was modified, deleted, or added. Have a look at the following screenshot:

A simple-to-follow color scheme helps you to identify data that has been modified, deleted, or added in between both the responses. Have a look at the following screenshot:

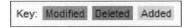

The top of the **Compare** window clearly indicates how many differences were detected by Burp. Have a look at the following screenshot:

Word compare of #1 and #2 (41 differences)

Alerts

Alerts is not a tool as such but a place for all suite-wide notifications that Burp might want to share. This is also a good place to see whether the proxy started successfully or faced any errors. Whenever there are issues with SSL negotiation for applications, the information on the errors, and others, they can be found in the **Alerts** tab. It is a good idea to check what is being listed here if something is not working for you.

Summary

In this chapter, we used some of the lesser-known Burp Suite tools, such as Comparer, Decoder, Sequencer, Spider, and briefly mentioned the **Alerts** tab. Even though these are not as widely used as the tools we saw in *Chapter 5, Using Burp Tools As a Power User – Part 1*, but an accomplished web application security tester can use these tools to do their testing in a more structured and efficient manner.

Now we know how to spider any application, break seemingly random tokens, compare different types of HTTP requests and responses, and decode and encode pieces of data as required for our testing and creating attacks.

In the next chapter, we will look at how to search, match patterns, and use grep-like tools in Burp Suite over requests and responses while we test the applications.

7
Searching, Extracting, Pattern Matching, and More

There are thousands of different types of web applications with hundreds of thousands of features and functionality. The suite of tools provided by Burp are quite powerful in terms of doing the heavy lifting of crafting HTTP requests and responses based on our actions on the web applications. An important aspect of that power is the ability to match, extract, find, grep, and search all these requests and responses based on our requirements.

In this chapter, we will learn the various ways in which we can search, extract, and pattern match data in requests and responses, which will allow us to complete our testing.

The ability to search and filter is provided throughout the application. Most editors show a search bar at the bottom for quick search of text, as shown in the following screenshot:

We can select different options to specify whether we would like to ignore the case, use regular expressions, or scroll with each occurrence of the string found:

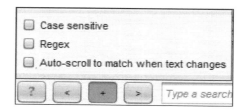

In theoretical computer science and formal language theory, a regular expression (abbreviated **regex** or **regexp**), sometimes called a rational expression, is a sequence of characters that forms a search pattern, mainly for use in pattern matching with strings, or string matching, that is *find and replace-like* operations. Each character in a regular expression is either understood to be a metacharacter with its special meaning or a regular character with its literal meaning—from Wikipedia http://en.wikipedia.org/wiki/Regular_expression.

Regular expressions are an extremely powerful tool for anyone working regularly with text. Covering regular expressions here is beyond the scope of this book, but being familiar with regular expressions is quite important for security testers.

A great resource for you to get started with regular expressions is: http://www.regular-expressions.info/

Filtering

While searching for text is useful, sometimes the amount of data presented becomes overwhelming. Especially, since we are using Burp to assist us in assessments, we need to be able to quickly filter and pay attention to what is relevant and ignore what is not.

In the **Target Site map**, we have a comprehensive display filter. Using the filter options, we can zero in to the exact requests that are of interest to us and hide all that is not. Have a look at the following screenshot:

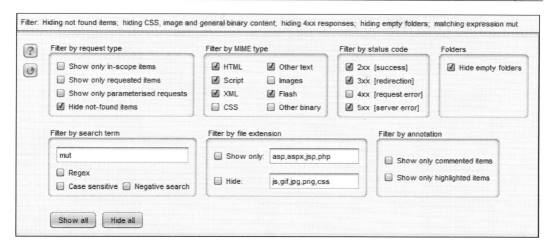

In this comprehensive display filter, we can do many different kinds of filtering based on our requirements and what it is that we are trying to analyze.

We can filter using the following options:

- Request type to show only in-scope requests, show only parameterized requests, and even hide items not found, as shown in the following screenshot:

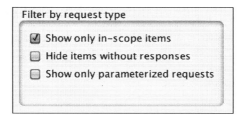

- Filtering by MIME type so that, based on our context, we can ignore images, cascading style sheets, and other HTML pages. None of the options are selected by default. Have a look at the following screenshot:

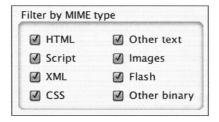

- Filtering by HTTP status codes is shown in the following screenshot:

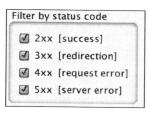

- Hide empty folders.

- Filtering by annotation is shown in the following screenshot. This is useful if we have already highlighted certain requests and/or added comments, and we just want to look at those:

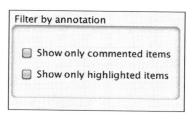

- File extension with options of show only and hide are another set of options. We can add more extensions separated by commas. Based on what we are after, we can show and/or hide the extensions that are not important for analysis currently, as shown in the following screenshot:

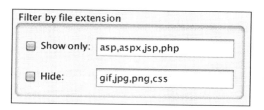

- Filtering by search term. Here, we can specify a simple text-only search term or even a regular expression. Have a look at the following screenshot:

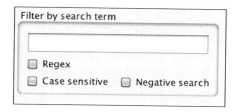

A simple **Reset** button just under the **Help** button allows us to reset the values to default if we need to do that.

Illustration

When we load Mutillidae for the first time in our browser, we get 28 HTTP requests and responses. By the time we log in as any user, the request and response count goes up to 37. If the objective was to fuzz the login form and you don't want to see all the filtered requests, you can use the following settings to zero in on the data that is useful to us.

By careful selection of options in the display filter, we can bring down the number of requests and responses we want to work with to 1 or 2. Have a look at the following screenshot:

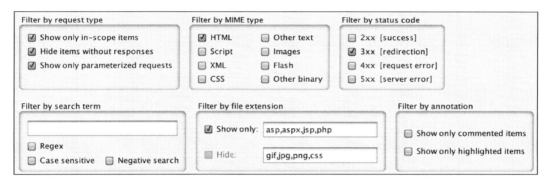

Matching

Filtering makes for a powerful analysis tool. But filtering happens after the requests have been sent, the responses received, and we just need to analyze the output. What if we want to make changes on the fly? Ideally, we would like to match certain data, such as requests, responses, parameter values, header values, and more. So, while the HTTP requests and responses are going through and coming back, we can create rules to match the data and perform operations on that data.

Let's look at all the places we can perform matching and related operations:

- In the **Proxy | Options** tab:
    ○ Under **Intercept Client Requests**
    ○ Under **Intercept Server Responses**
    ○ Under **Match and Replace**

- In **Spider | Options**:
  - ° **Form Submission**

- In **Scanner | Options**:
  - ° **Attack Insertion Points**

- In **Intruder | Payloads**:
  - ° **Payloads Processing**

We can set rules for intercepting client requests based on conditions. Basically, a rule has a Boolean operator, a match type, a relationship based on the match type, and the condition. By default, certain rules are already set up for us. We can choose to enable or disable these and add our own if required, as shown in following screenshot:

Enabled	Operator	Match type	Relationship	Condition
☑		File extension	Does not match	(^gif$|^jpg$|^png$|^css$|^js$|^ico$)
☐	Or	Request	Contains parameters	
☐	Or	HTTP method	Does not match	(get|post)
☐	And	URL	Is in target scope	

The rule creator for intercepting server responses is quite like the one mentioned in the following screenshot:

Enabled	Operator	Match type	Relationship	Condition
☑		Content type header	Matches	text
☐	Or	Request	Was modified	
☑	Or	Request	Was intercepted	
☐	And	Status code	Does not match	^304$
☐	And	URL	Is in target scope	

By default, the setting to intercept server responses is not enabled. It is useful to enable this with an additional rule to only intercept a server response if the corresponding request was intercepted as well.

Match and Replace is useful when we want to change or replace some data in requests or responses when it passes through the proxy. Have a look at the following screenshot:

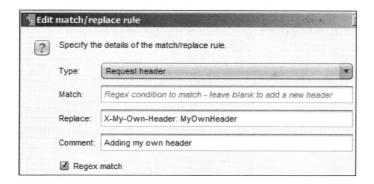

We can even add a new header using the special match/replace rules editor. Just by leaving the **Match** field blank and adding the relevant header in the **Replace** field, we can easily add our header. This will show up in the automodified request.

Another useful trick is to match and replace the default user agent of the browser to emulate another browser or a mobile device:

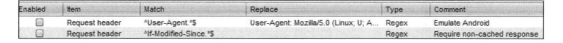

Enabled	Item	Match	Replace	Type	Comment
☐	Request header	^User-Agent.*$	User-Agent: Mozilla/5.0 (Linux; U; A...	Regex	Emulate Android
☐	Request header	^If-Modified-Since.*$		Regex	Require non-cached response

Just by enabling a default rule for matching the **User-Agent** header, we can replace the current browser and emulate an Android device. This can easily be another mobile device or whatever we need to bypass a user-agent check. We can also try to make the remote web application reveal new functionalities that usually are exposed to specific devices only — and so, try to correctly map the application's attack surface.

Similarly in the **Spider** options, we can match form fields to allow us to add our customized data while submitting forms automatically. In **Scanner Options**, under **Attack insertion points**, we can skip injection tests for some standard acceptable parameters and even add our own. Have a look at the following screenshot:

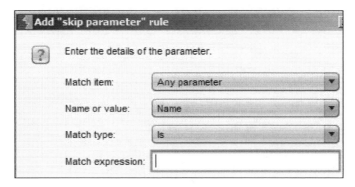

Just like all the other places, we can match the exact string or a regular expression. In **Intruder | Payloads** under payload processing, we can set match/replace rules as well. Have a look at the following screenshot:

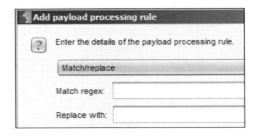

This operation will work on each payload that we specify before.

Grep - Match and Grep - Extract

Grep is the simplest and most used command-line tool on Linux/Unix to match and extract data based on patterns, which can be simple string comparisons or regular expressions.

We can use **Grep - Match** to quickly identify requests/responses that we get in the **Intruder** results to filter these results based on certain conditions. Matches are shown in a new column, which we can sort to quickly make sense of the output.

The default values provided to us are good to use, and we can add more based on our requirement. Have a look at the following screenshot:

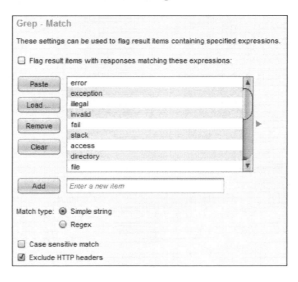

We can add more keywords, set the match type to be simple strings or regular expression patterns, and load more from our list of keywords. It is great for analysis of output from the **Intruder** tool!

Grep - Extract allows us to extract data using the response extraction rules for the requests made in **Intruder**. As in **Grep - Match**, a new column will list extracted data in a new column. Response extraction is useful in many cases, such as the following examples from the Burp documentation:

- Given a list of document IDs, extracting document titles for further analysis
- Given a list of usernames, extracting unique password hints per user

The **Grep - Extract** interface looks like this:

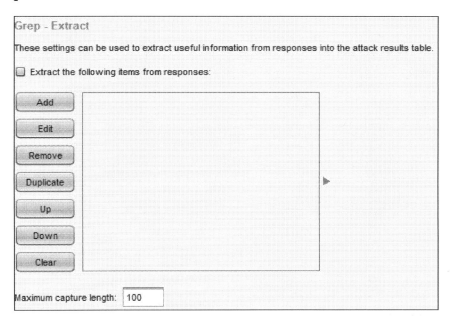

We can and should always set **Maximum capture length** to a reasonable number.

Summary

From this chapter, we have a good idea about how the various tools of Burp Suite can be supercharged with effective searching, filtering, and matching of data. Based on simple strings and many times with regular expressions, we can do better analysis of data already generated, or customize our requests and responses to manipulate the applications. We also saw that **Match and Replace** is an incredibly powerful operation that allows us to add/remove headers and other data and even emulate mobile devices on the fly.

Grep - Match allows us to gain more control over the output of the **Intruder** tool, which is a blessing because the **Intruder** tool can generate a lot of data and manually trawling through that would not be too productive. **Grep - Extract** allows us to not only match the data, but also extract it for further analysis and operations.

Next, we look at the Burp Suite Pro features called engagement tools. We will look at how these tools can be used cohesively to make our security-testing engagement smoother and more efficient.

8
Using Engagement Tools and Other Utilities

Engagement tools is a Pro-only feature of Burp Suite. Apart from the engagement tools, we will look at some smaller utilities that aid the testing process, such as Search, Target Analyzer, Content Discovery, Task Scheduler, CSRF PoC Generator, and Manual Testing Simulator.

Out of all these, Manual Testing Simulator doesn't really have any use except maybe like an inside joke for the creators. But it is enabled and can be used. The idea behind all the other tools is to make the testing process smoother and faster. These tools enhance the testing process, but due to their nature, they can be time consuming and boring when done manually. Since they are of lower priority, we might give them a miss, but the Burp Suite Pro version helps us to ensure that we go ahead and complete them.

In the free version of Burp Suite, the engagement tool context menu is disabled with a message that this is meant for the Pro version only, as shown in the following screenshot:

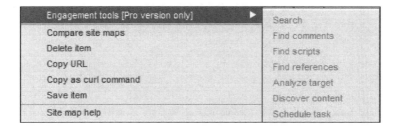

In the Pro version, we can see many options for **Engagement tools** in the context menu, as shown in the following screenshot:

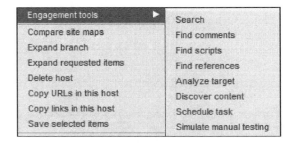

In this chapter, we will cover Search, Target Analyzer, Content Discovery, Task Scheduler, and Manual Testing Simulator.

Search

Search is one of the key interfaces when working with Burp Suite. This works well for most of us who are already familiar with search being the primary interface to find information on the web. The advantage of using **Search** as an interface is the fact that we stop caring about how much information is available to us as long as we are able to find the relevant information reliably and reasonably quickly.

To begin searching, we just need to go to **Burp | Search** in the menu bar. This provides us with a suite-wide search scope. Have a look at the following screenshot:

The search form is quite simple to understand. Any result that matches the simple text search will be returned from Target, Proxy, Scanner, and Repeater. As usual, we can use regular expressions, choose to negate the match, search only for in-scope items, and ignore case as well. The search will apply to all headers and body requests and responses. Have a look at the following screenshot:

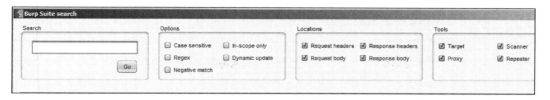

In the **Target Site map** context menu, you can search only for comments. Sometimes, developers leave information that can be revealing for the application. Burp Suite can find all the HTML comments on all the pages it can see and lets you go through these quickly.

We can export the comments as well for further analysis or add them as part of our report. **Dynamic update** allows us to automatically update the search results based on our term if more responses contain the term. Take a look at the following screenshot:

The **Export comments** and **Export scripts** wizards looks exactly the same. With options to deduplicate, save to clipboard or save to a file, and including the URLs in the report, both of them allow us to store and do further processing of comments and scripts:

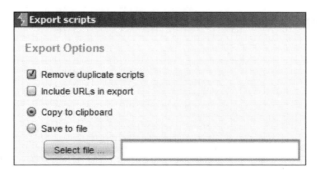

Target Analyzer

The Target Analyzer tool is the perfect example of an engagement tool. Target Analyzer can help you to quickly figure out how many dynamic and static links you are dealing with in a website. It will also tell you how many parameters are required for each of the links. This can be utilized to calculate time and effort required to test the application. Additionally, this can give you a good idea as to what to test first, or what to focus on while starting the application. Do note that Target Analyzer only picks information from the site map, and it does not do any scanning of its own. So, we need to finish the task of mapping the application before we can analyze the target.

Target Analyzer shows the number of dynamic and static URLs. It also mentions the total number of parameters it was able to see, as shown in the following screenshot:

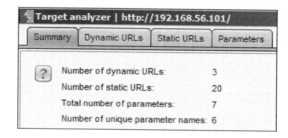

Under the **Dynamic URLs** tab, we can see the complete list of dynamic URLs. Similarly, under **Static URLs**, we can see all the listed static URLs. Obviously, under the **Parameters** tab, we can see all the parameters found so far, as shown in the following screenshot:

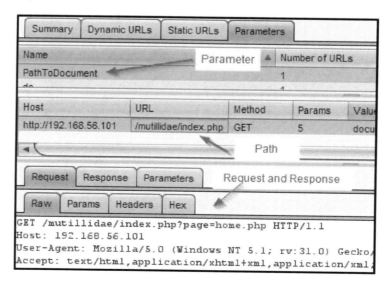

In the **Parameters** tab, we can see each and every unique parameter listed with a list of paths where that parameter was found. Also, we can see the exact request and response that uses the parameter.

Content Discovery

How do you find a directory that is not linked by any page in the application? If we know the directory name, we can check for its existence by making a request for it. A HTTP status code of **200** and **403** will quickly tell us that the directory, in fact, exists but is not linked anywhere. Similarly, there are many techniques to discover content.

> Depending on how a web application is created, Content Discovery can be quite useful or utterly useless. Some applications might return HTTP status code **200** even for resources that are not found. So, we need to be smart about the results. Also what we can do with Content Discovery can be achieved by using Intruder as well. Testers normally use other discovery tools such as OWASP DirBuster and Nikto along with Burp Suite.

To get started, in the Pro version of Burp Suite, we can right-click on any HTTP request under **Engagement tools** and click on the **Discover Content** option. The same action can be performed in **Target Site map** as well.

Burp Suite uses different techniques to discover content, including brute-forcing file and folder names. First, we define the starting path for Content Discovery and specify if we are after files and directories or only files:

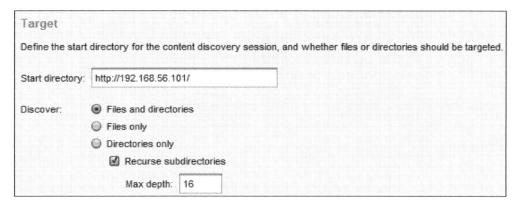

There is a built-in list for filenames and directory names. Burp can reuse any file and directory names it finds during discovery and add them to the list. So, if recursive testing is enabled, all the previously found names will be tested in each new directory found. Have a look at the following screenshot:

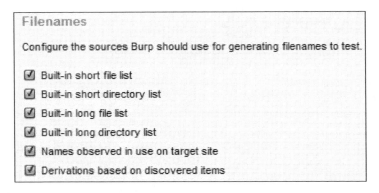

Additionally, we can specify which file extensions should be checked for and which should be ignored, and it is always worthwhile to search for file extensions that ideally should never be inside the document root of any web application:

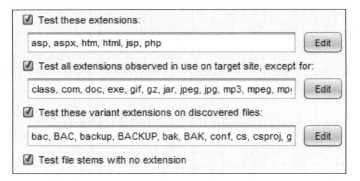

We can choose to send the output of discovered content to be added to the main **Target Site map** and spidered for more discovery.

At this point, we are all set to discover the content. This is handled by the **Control** tab. Once we are all prepared, click on the **Session is not running** button and Content Discovery will start. A few statistics update while the session for Content Discovery is running:

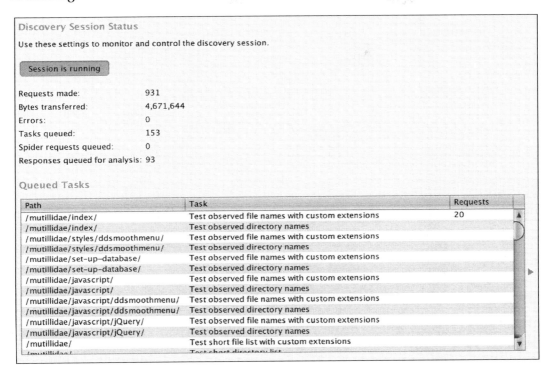

Task Scheduler

Burp Suite provides the handy Task Scheduler for a few tools that can be quite useful depending on your use case.

A common task to schedule is an automatic backup of the Burp Suite session. We cover this in detail in *Chapter 10, Saving Securely, Backing Up, and Other Maintenance Activities*.

Sometimes, clients have strict requirements as to what times we are allowed to do security testing. Task Scheduler allows you to start, resume, pause scanning, and spidering.

We can schedule tasks under the engagement tools or go to **Suite Options | Misc** under **Schedule Tasks**. Have a look at the following screenshot:

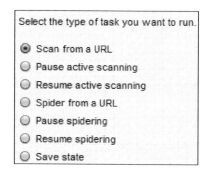

Once we select the type of task, we choose the date and time to start the task. We can also specify the interval. The interval can be in days, hours, or minutes, as shown in the following screenshot:

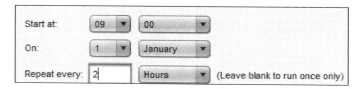

Now that the task has been scheduled, if we want to add, edit, or remove scheduled tasks, we need to go to **Suite Options | Misc | Scheduled Tasks**. Take a look at the following screenshot:

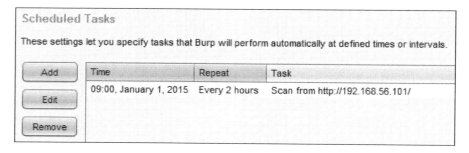

CSRF proof of concept Generator

CSRF **proof of concept (PoC)** Generator is the most useful nonessential tool provided by the Pro version of Burp Suite. This simply takes any request and automatically writes the HTML code for doing a PoC for cross-site request forgery.

 Cross-site request forgery is mentioned in the OWASP top-10 risks applications face. Any security testing of a web application without checking for CSRF defenses is incomplete. Burp Suite does the grunt work of generating a PoC HTML page that can be used by the tester to see whether the application checks for CSRF defenses, such as a valid token.

All we have to do is choose a HTTP request, right-click on it, and navigate to **Engagement tools | Generate CSRF PoC**.

The ideal candidate for CSRF testing would be a POST request, which doesn't have any CSRF token checks being implemented. The CSRF PoC Generator not only creates the HTML code for us, but it can also generate the required JavaScript to autosubmit the form. Have a look at the following screenshot:

```html
<html>
  <!-- CSRF PoC - generated by Burp Suite Professional -->
  <body>
    <form action="http://owaspbwa/mutillidae/index.php?page=add-to-your-blog.php"
    method="POST">
      <input type="hidden" name="csrf&#45;token" value="SecurityIsDisabled" />
      <input type="hidden" name="blog&#95;entry" value="Testing&#32;123" />
      <input type="hidden" name="add&#45;to&#45;your&#45;blog&#45;php&#45;submit&
#45;button" value="Save&#32;Blog&#32;Entry" />
      <input type="submit" value="Submit request" />
    </form>
    <script>
    document.forms[0].submit();
    </script>
  </body>
</html>
```

There are other options that can be used, but in most cases, the CSRF technique autoselected works very well for the generation of the PoC. If you make any changes in the options, the code needs to be generated again using the **Regenerate** button provided in the bottom-left corner of the tool's window. Have a look at the following screenshot:

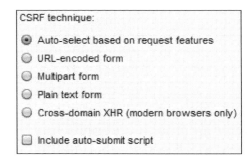

Do remember to click on **Regenerate** after every option change, as shown in the following screenshot:

Summary

In this chapter, we saw some smaller tools that are part of the Pro version of Burp Suite. Even though we could do without these tools, they make working with clients, reporting, and so on, easy. We looked at suite-wide search functionality, how we can find comments and scripts in web pages, how we can analyze a target that can aid in estimating our testing effort, and additional discovery of content that is not linked anywhere by the brute-forcing file and directory names. We also looked at how we can schedule tasks and repeat them and how we can generate PoCs for CSRF.

Most of these tasks can be done manually, and a lot of us end up doing that; with the automation provided by Burp Suite, we can ensure quality and consistency of these tasks, which are low priority, but can make a great testing assessment even better.

In the next chapter, we will look at how we can extend the core functionality of Burp Suite with extensions using the Burp Suite Extender tool.

9

Using Burp Extensions and Writing Your Own

Not only does Burp Suite come with its own rich set of tools, it also provides API interfaces to extend its functionality. Many security researchers have written extensions that enhance the native functionality or add to the already rich tool set.

Using the **Extender** tool, we can load and manage different extensions written for Burp Suite. These extensions might extend the core functionality of Burp Suite or provide an easy way to do something that might be difficult with the basic Burp Suite tools.

Burp Suite comes with its own BApp Store, which contains different types of extensions that are ready to load and use. A few extensions are only meant for the Pro version. The BApp Store is also available online, and the extensions can be downloaded and installed manually if required (`https://pro.portswigger.net/bappstore/`).

Burp Extensions can be written in Java, Python, or Ruby. For Python and Ruby, we need to set up the environment before we can start using these extensions.

Let's see how to do all that in this chapter.

Setting up the Python runtime for Burp Extensions

To set up the Python runtime for Burp Extensions, perform the following steps:

1. Download a stable version of Jython standalone JAR file from `http://mirrors.ibiblio.org/maven2/org/python/jython-standalone/2.5.3/`.
2. Save the file to `E:\jython\jython-standalone-2.5.3.jar`.
3. Configure the path in **Extender | Options | Python Environment**.
4. We are all set to run Python-based Burp Extensions now.

 Do note that the path for the Jython file depends on where you download it in your machine.

Similarly, we can easily set up the Ruby environment required to run Burp Extensions written in Ruby.

Setting up the Ruby environment for Burp Extensions

Let's follow these steps to set up the Ruby environment:

1. Download a stable version of JRuby from `http://www.jruby.org/download`.
2. Download **JRuby 1.7.15 Binary .zip** and unzip this file. Inside the `lib` folder, you will find `jruby.jar`.
3. Copy this to `E:\jruby\jruby.jar`.
4. Configure the path through **Extender | Options| Ruby Environment**.

 Note that the path for JRuby depends on where you download JRuby in your machine.

We can also add the path of additional libraries required for Java-based extensions in the same place.

Before Burp Version 1.5.01+, getting extensions was not straightforward and consistent. Since the introduction of the Burp app store, it has become very convenient to load and install new extensions.

The obvious limitation is that the extension author needs to submit the extension to get it added to the Burp app store. Currently, this can be done by sending an e-mail to support@portswigger.com with the subject line Submit BApp.

Once the extension is featured, it will show up on the website or inside Burp Suite under the **BApp Store** subtab, as shown in the following screenshot:

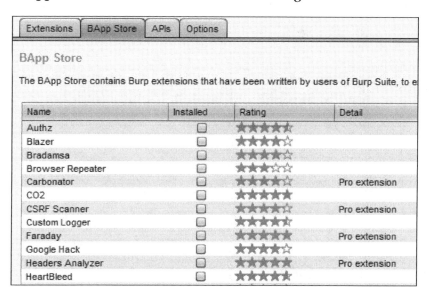

Loading and installing a Burp Extension from the Burp App Store

Getting and using Burp Extensions featured in the Burp App Store is just a series of simple steps we can easily follow:

1. Go to **Extender | BApp Store**, and select the extension you want to install from the list.

2. If the runtime is set up correctly, you will get an **Install** button, along with a description of the extension, author information, rating (five stars being the maximum).

3. Clicking on **Install** will initiate the downloading of the extension, and if all goes well, the **Install** button will turn into **Reinstall**.

4. The extension will get listed under Burp Extensions.

Using BApp files

If we want to install extensions in offline mode, we can do this using the manual installation method:

1. To do this, first we download the extension we want to install. Have a look at the following screenshot:

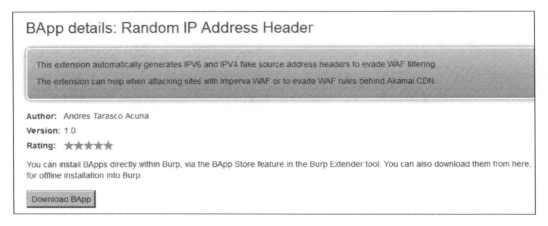

2. Click on the **Manual install** button provided at the bottom of the **BApp Store** tab. Browse to the folder where we downloaded the .bapp file. Have a look at the following screenshot:

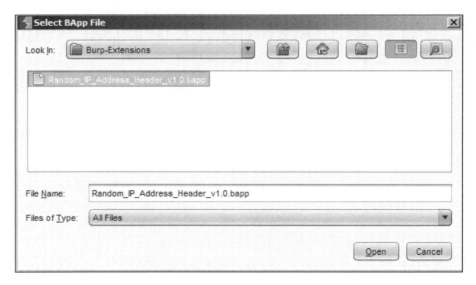

3. Opening this file will install the extension, and we can manage it like any other extension installed directly from the **BApp Store** tab.

Loading and installing a Burp Extension manually

Not all extensions are present in the BApp Store. In such a case, we need to download the extension files ourselves. To do this, use the **Add** button provided under the **Burp Extensions** section, and browse to the extension file:

In **Extension type**, we can choose **Java**, **Python**, or **Ruby**, and based on that, we need to browse to the actual extension file for the language we choose.

GitHub is a great place to find extensions. A simple text search will reveal different and interesting extensions being written by people all across the world:

```
https://github.com/search?utf8=%E2%9C%93&q=burp+extension
```

Managing Burp Extensions

All the extensions we install and load are visible under **Burp Extensions**. We can always remove the extension using the **Remove** button. We can modify the order in which we load the extensions. Have a look at the following screenshot:

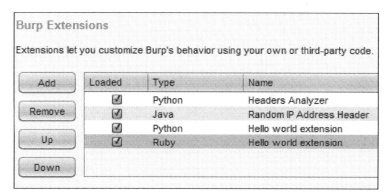

For each extension that gets loaded, we see more information below that. Have a look at the following screenshot:

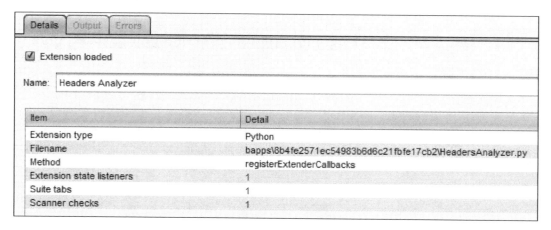

Based on the settings chosen, output and errors will show up in the UI, or they can be written to a local file.

Some of the extensions modify the standard tabs present in Burp. This is primarily in order to provide a user interface to edit various options offered by the extensions. Have a look at the following screenshot:

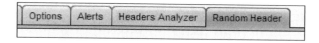

Apart from this, we need to refer to the documentation provided with the extension to understand if any specific Burp Suite tool has been enhanced by the extension or not.

For example, the **Headers Analyzer** extension (only available for the Pro version of Burp Suite) adds more information as part of the Scanner results by passively collating all kinds of response headers. Have a look at the following screenshot:

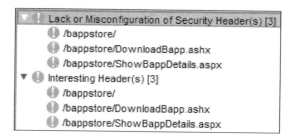

We can also configure the **Header Analyzer** extension with different options based on our requirements. Have a look at the following screenshot:

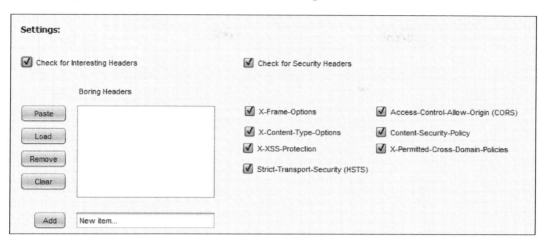

Memory issues with Burp Extensions

While loading, unloading, and adding extensions, you might encounter memory issues. This is a known issue, and guidance has been provided to ensure that this does not affect our work. Whenever you encounter errors such as the one shown in the following screenshot, you need to take some additional steps while starting Burp.

The following screenshot shows the Java out-of-memory error since we are loading and unloading multiple extensions:

```
java.lang.OutOfMemoryError: PermGen space
        at java.lang.ClassLoader.defineClass1(Native Method)
        at java.lang.ClassLoader.defineClass(Unknown Source)
        at java.security.SecureClassLoader.defineClass(Unknown Source)
        at java.net.URLClassLoader.defineClass(Unknown Source)
```

This happens due to the way Jython and JRuby dynamically generate Java classes, so loading many extensions can cause this to happen.

We can use the following command-line flag to ensure that enough memory is available to dynamically generate Java classes, which is required for loading multiple Burp Extensions:

```
java -XX:MaxPermSize=1G -jar burp.jar
```

Writing our own Burp Extensions

Writing your own Burp Extensions is a great way to understand how the Burp Suite software works. As mentioned earlier, we can write extensions in Java, Python, and Ruby by simply setting up the environment correctly.

 There is a project by Lift Security, called burpbuddy, that exposes a certain functionality of Burp and allows the creation of extensions in any language without the restrictions of JVM. For more information on this, visit `https://github.com/ liftsecurity/burpbuddy`.

The best place to get started with writing extensions is to read the following blog post:

`http://blog.portswigger.net/2012/12/writing-your-first-burp- extension.html`

The step-by-step process with the basic template code explains what it takes to write your own extension and load it on Burp Suite.

A simple Burp Extension in Python

Let's write a simple Burp Extension in Python. In terms of functionality, the extension won't do much, but will print the headers of a request if the method is POST and return the status code of the response. Have a look at the following code:

```
# All extensions need to import IBurpExtender
from burp import IBurpExtender

# This will allow us to start a HTTP Listener
from burp import IHttpListener

# This will allow us to retrieve and update details about HTTP
messages.
from burp import IHttpRequestResponse

# The following two will allow us to get more details about requests
and responses
from burp import IRequestInfo
from burp import IResponseInfo

# Basic debugging by printing to standard output
from java.io import PrintWriter
```

```python
class BurpExtender(IBurpExtender,IHttpListener,IHttpRequestResponse,I
RequestInfo):

    def registerExtenderCallbacks(self, callbacks):
        # This function is required to setup callbacks and get access
        to helper functions.
        self._callbacks = callbacks
        self._helpers = callbacks.getHelpers()

        # This is where you name your extension. This name will show
        under Extensions | Burp Extensions when loaded.
        callbacks.setExtensionName("My first Burp extension")

        self._stdout = PrintWriter(callbacks.getStdout(), True)

        callbacks.registerHttpListener(self)

        # This will get printed once the extension is loaded without
        any errors
        self._stdout.println("Hello, Burp Extension World!")

        return

    def processHttpMessage(self, toolFlag, messageIsRequest,
    messageInfo):
        # This function is where all the work happens for us.

        # We want to ensure that we are working with a request to
        begin with.
        if messageIsRequest:
            requestInfo = self._helpers.analyzeRequest(messageInfo)

            # We are interested in finding out when a HTTP POST
            request is made.
            if requestInfo.getMethod() == "POST":
                # Once we have determined that an HTTP POST request
                was made, we want to enumerate the headers.
                headers = requestInfo.getHeaders()

                # Use the next line for debugging, if required.
                #self._stdout.println("Printing Request")
```

```
# We are trying to find the Header Content-Type and
then search for a form that has upload capabilities
for header in headers:
    if header.startswith("Content-Type:") and
    "multipart/form-data" in header:
        # This comment will be useful for us later
        when we look for all kinds of requests,
        messageInfo.setComment("File Upload detected
        and this comment was created by an extension.")

        # Print all the headers
        self._stdout.println(header)

else:
    # Since we didn't get a request, we will look at response.
    responseInfo = self._helpers.analyzeResponse(self._
    helpers.bytesToString(messageInfo.getResponse()))

    # Many times, we figure out next steps based on the status
    code of the response.
    self._stdout.println(responseInfo.getStatusCode())
```

The Burp Suite website offers more code snippets with examples to try out basic functionalities, including a simple extension that outputs **Hello World**.

The `EventListeners` extension with sample code is a great way to learn how to process HTTP messages, proxy messages, new scan issues, and more:

http://blog.portswigger.net/2012/12/sample-burp-suite-extension-event.html

The `BurpExtensions` website has a simple-to-follow tutorial to create an extension written in Python, which activates a UI change for a certain type of header when it is found in a HTTP response:

http://www.burpextensions.com/tutorials/tutorial-python-extension-post-1/

The full code can be downloaded from http://www.burpextensions.com/downloads/pythontutorial-1.txt.

Noteworthy Burp Extensions

The following are some of the extensions worth taking a look at:

- **Heartbleed**: This extension checks whether a particular server is vulnerable to the Heartbleed vulnerability (`http://heartbleed.com`). Usually, such a check would be done by the vulnerability assessment software, such as Nessus or Nmap with NSE.

- **Logger++**: Many times, a client report requires full logs of each and every request and response. Logger++ takes care of this really well. The logs can be sorted and also saved in CSV format, which can then be imported in a spreadsheet software, such as Microsoft Excel or OpenOffice Calc.

- **CO2**: This extension has multiple features, of which the most useful one for me is the ability to give the sqlmap command-line output that can be directly run on the command line.

- **Reissue Request scripter**: This extension generates scripts from **Proxy history**, which can then be saved outside of Burp and run from the command line. These scripts are generated for Python, Ruby, Perl, PHP, and PowerShell and are mainly to test for second-order SQL injection and padding Oracle vulnerabilities.

> This extension gives us the ability to store text notes while doing the assessment. Many testers have different ways of storing such information, but the ability to store information in the tool itself is useful in many cases.

There are many other extensions that might be useful for certain cases. Until very recently, Burp Suite didn't have great support for static analysis of JavaScript for DOM XSS detection (however, Burp Suite now supports DOM XSS identification), and a bunch of people have written extensions for that. There are extensions to beautify JavaScript (many websites compress them for various reasons) and .NET. Some extensions are written to send the Scanner data to external systems from where they can be scanned again or kept just for the record.

Summary

Now we are in a position to work with Burp Extensions. Extensions are meant to enhance and extend the functionality or at times complement its event. Nowadays, Burp has the Burp App Store, and extensions can be installed and loaded in a structured manner. Extension authors can also distribute their extensions to a wider audience once their extensions are in the Burp App Store.

If you encounter cases where the tools provided by Burp and the extensions aren't enough, you can write your own extensions in Java, Python, and Ruby. For example, you can passively scan for error messages, connect with PhantomJS to validate XSS findings, audit HTML5 security, and do much more. Using tools such as burpbuddy, you can even write them in other languages that you might think of.

The next chapter is all about maintenance activities required when we do real-world security testing. We'll learn how we save our sessions, backup, and more.

10
Saving Securely, Backing Up, and Other Maintenance Activities

Burp Suite is just like any software a knowledge worker will use. Users of the tool, like you and me, use the tool to work on some data and come up with more data. All the work that we do and the output of our efforts should be secured and backed up like any other person who works with spreadsheets or document software.

In this chapter, we will see what features Burp Suite has to save our work, back up our data while we are busy doing security testing, and any other maintenance activities that we should take up as part of good security testing project hygiene.

First and foremost is the fact that we want to be able to save the state of our current session. This feature is only available in the Pro version of the software, so the free users are left hanging here. Have a look at the following screenshot:

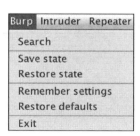

The following is what Burp Suite Free users see instead:

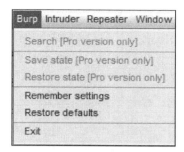

A few security geeks get past this clear limitation by running Burp and OWASP ZAP together. So, ZAP can be used to save and restore the session. All Burp traffic will be proxied to OWASP ZAP. This technique is well documented in Justin Searle's *Samurai WTF Course Slides* at `http://sourceforge.net/projects/samurai/files/SamuraiWTF%20Course/`.

The steps to do this are fairly simple and straightforward, as follows:

1. Add an upstream proxy in Burp Suite under the **Options | Connections** tab.
2. The **Proxy host** will be `127.0.0.1`, and the port needs to match where OWASP ZAP will listen.
3. Start OWASP ZAP and choose **File | Persist Session**.
4. Edit the **Port** value in the **Local proxy** setting to match the value given to Burp Suite. You can reach the settings in the menu item by navigating to **Tools | Options**.
5. Now all the requests and responses will get saved in OWASP ZAP session.

Saving and restoring a state

Once we start relying on Burp Suite Pro for all our application security testing, we need to ensure that we are safely able to save and restore all the work that we are doing.

Now, based on your workload, you might be working on only one application at a time, or you might have to test different applications for the same or different clients. Either way, a good idea is to completely separate the state and configuration for each application.

Saving the state allows you to close the Burp session at the end of the day.

We can save the current state of **Target, Proxy, Scanner,** and **Repeater**. A great option is to save the state for only in-scope items. Have a look at the following screenshot:

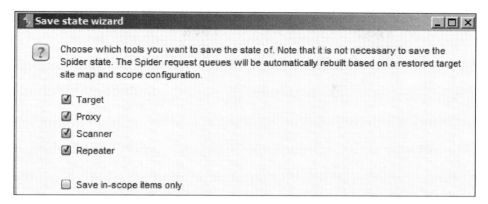

While we can only save the state of four tools, we can save all our configuration settings for almost all of the tools:

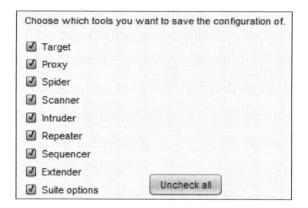

Apart from saving the configuration settings, we should save all sensitive information, such as passwords, with a master password. Needless to say, this password should be strong:

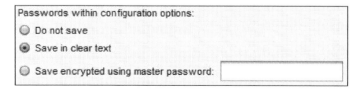

There is no way to save the state for Intruder. What you can do is save the attack configurations with payloads. Have a look at the following screenshot:

The restore wizard works like the save wizard. We can choose what to restore and what not to restore. Have a look at the following screenshot:

We can choose the tools that should have their configuration restored as well. By default, the configuration is **Pause Spider and Scanner after restore**. This makes sense as we may not be ready to resume a scan just after a restore. Sometimes, we might be restoring after the project is over, but we need to look at some of results to answer client questions. In such cases, automatic scanning is a bad idea. Have a look at the following screenshot:

Automatic backups

We can and should back up our work in Burp. We can set this as an automated action in Suite **Options** | **Misc** under **Automatic Backup**.

This option has saved my life and sanity multiple times. When I just started using Burp and was unaware of setting memory options while starting a few times, I had the software crash on me. This feature is incredibly useful if your work becomes part of a report that might be seen by others.

Two sensible options, along with enabling automatic backups, are to choose a folder on a partition with enough free disk space, and ideally backup only in-scope elements.

I personally back up the folder to an external drive using my operating system backup program just in case there is a catastrophic disk failure. Have a look at the following screenshot:

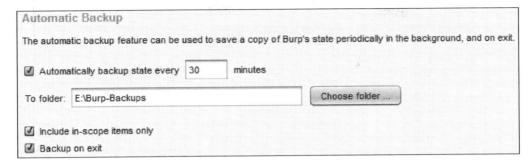

Scheduled tasks

There is a scheduled task we can run to save the state. Automatic backups are great, but sometimes, there is more assurance in saving the state at regular intervals to ensure that we do not lose our precious testing work. Take a look at the following screenshot:

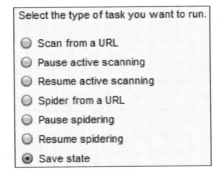

As usual, we should save the state for in-scope items on a drive that has ample free disk space:

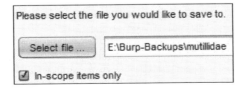

Based on the amount of scanning, Spidering, and other activities you are doing, you might want to figure out a good time interval to repeat. 60 minutes seems like decent enough time, but you might want to lower or increase this based on your comfort level. Have a look at the following screenshot:

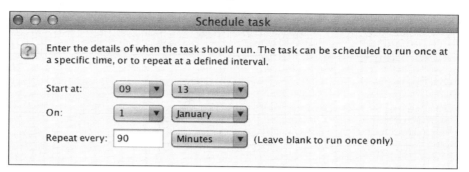

Logging all activities

Under Suite **Options** | **Misc** | **Logging**, we get the option to log each and every HTTP request and response for the different tools that are part of Burp Suite.

Logging all requests and responses might be a client requirement or may be that you prefer keeping complete records of all requests and responses made. Even though this may not be required always, it is very reassuring to know that, if required, we can trace all the requests and responses we made using the tool sometime in the future. Have a look at the following screenshot:

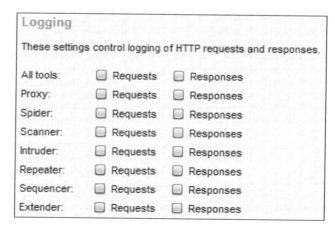

Summary

In this chapter, we saw how to go about creating a basic process for data backup and configuration backup. This is done via saving the state of the application and being able to restore the same state. This is a Pro-only feature, but some testers figured out how to chain Burp Suite and OWASP ZAP to get similar functionality with the free version of Burp. We also looked at automatic backup of data, scheduled saving of state, and logging functionality for all HTTP requests and responses.

Burp Suite provides enough tools for most of us to create a robust backup and recovery strategy if we ever need it. Keeping the data of all projects separate and password-protected is a good way to ensure that no leakage happens and that mistakes don't cause any irreversible issues for us.

We have almost reached the end. The next chapter will cover all the helpful and wonderful resources and links available to use and work with Burp Suite.

11

Resources, References, and Links

Burp is a great piece of software. If you are still reading, then you think so, too. The biggest feature of the suite is the fact that it gets out of the way of the user while testing. While there is a recommended workflow we can use for testing, testers need not follow it always. Some of the features are discovered over time and with experience. While this is great, it also means that there is a learning curve.

This book offers you a start, but there are a lot of great resources and references that you should rely on as well. We will look at the primary references that you should follow to get more insights and approaches into how web security practitioners use Burp. We will also list useful and informative resources for application security as well.

Primary references

The Burp Suite documentation is the primary reference for this book, and it should be the primary reference for anyone planning to use Burp or even if you have been using Burp Suite for some time.

Learning about Burp

The primary source for all the Burp-related documentation has to be the documentation that is shipped with the product and what is present on the website:

- You can always get the latest documentation online at http://portswigger.net/burp/help/.

- You might prefer having a handy table of contents, found at http://portswigger.net/burp/help/contents.html.

- All the help available online is also part of Burp Suite. You can access it using the **Help** menu:

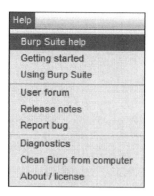

- The **Troubleshooting** page is always useful:
  `http://portswigger.net/burp/help/suite_troubleshooting.html`
- The user forums on the website are useful when facing issues where the regular documentation isn't helpful: `http://forum.portswigger.net/`
- A few video tutorials from the creators of Burp Suite can be viewed:
  `http://portswigger.net/burp/tutorials/`
- The PortSwigger blog on application security:
  `http://blog.portswigger.net/`

Web application security testing with Burp

Just learning about Burp is part of the job done. To gain understanding and to be able to apply the learning to accomplish real-world security testing tasks requires us to learn about web application security testing with Burp, as follows:

- All users of Burp should definitely read this *Pentesting with Burp Suite* presentation, `http://repo.zenk-security.com/Techniques%20d.attaques%20%20.%20%20Failles/Pentesting%20With%20Burp%20Suite.pdf`. This presentation is great to help a security tester understand how to use Burp Suite's capabilities for a web application penetration testing process. It's a great overview that is worth reading over and over again.

- *Burp Suite Pro – Real-life tips & tricks* is a great presentation on learning some tips and tricks that are useful while doing web application pentesting, `http://www.agarri.fr/docs/HiP2k13-Burp_Pro_Tips_and_Tricks.pdf`. This presentation tries to cover use cases that we may not encounter every day while using Burp Suite but covers great tips that we may use at some point.

- *Burp Suite Tutorial – Web Application Penetration Testing* is a good overview of the entire software, `https://www.pentestgeek.com/2014/07/02/burp-suite-tutorial-1/`.

- The *Hacking Web Services with Burp* article: `https://www.netspi.com/blog/entryid/57/hacking-web-services-with-burp`.

Miscellaneous security testing tutorials with Burp Suite

Other tutorials can be found at the following links:

- Security Ninja's tutorials on Burp Suite are very comprehensive and easy to follow, `http://www.securityninja.co.uk/?s=Burp+Suite`.

- The *Automating SQL Injection with Burp, Sqlmap, and GDS Burp API* article, `http://milo2012.wordpress.com/2012/06/26/automating-sql-injection-with-burp-sqlmap-and-gds-burp-api/`. sqlmap is the go-to tool for detecting and exploiting SQL injection. It is free and open source, and using Burp Suite with sqlmap is a brilliant idea. Find possible SQL injections with Burp Suite, and then pass them on to sqlmap for further analysis and attack.

- The *Adding Anti-CSRF Support to Burp Suite Intruder* blog post, `http://blog.spiderlabs.com/2012/09/adding-anti-csrf-support-to-burp-suite-intruder.html`. This particular blog post explains a real-world scenario, wherein using the Extender tool, we can supercharge the features of Burp Suite. The language is simple and the code is easy to understand. Even though this particular functionality can be implemented using **Macros** in Burp Suite, the whole thought process of the author is helpful.

- Data extraction can be done using the Burp Suite Intruder tool, and more information about this can be found at `http://blog.nvisium.com/2014/08/intro-to-burpsuite-v-extracting.html`. A step-by-step tutorial to using Burp Suite Intruder and stealing data from a vulnerable application using OWASP is available at Webgoat.net.

- The *Advanced XSS detection with BurpSuite and PhantomJS* blog post, `http://blog.nvisium.com/2014/01/accurate-xss-detection-with-burpsuite.html`. PhantomJS is a headless JavaScript environment. This post explains how to use PhantomJS to execute and test XSS integrated with Burp Suite.

- Browser fuzzing with Burp and Radamsa: `https://github.com/ikkisoft/bradamsa`.

- We can use FuzzDB with Burp Suite based on the information found at `http://www.securityninja.co.uk/application-security/improve-your-security-testing-with-the-fuzzdb/`. Combining the awesome FuzzDB test cases with Burp Suite, FuzzDB contains attack patterns, predictable resource locations, web shells, and more. All the tools that you can use with Burp Suite Intruder.

- *Taking Dirbuster Output into Burp Suite*: `http://www.securityaegis.com/taking-dirbuster-output-into-burp-suite/`.

- SQL injection with Burp Suite is an older tutorial but full of good information at `http://kaoticcreations.blogspot.in/2011/11/burp-suite-part-i-intro-via-sql.html`.

- *Automating Burp Security Scanning with BDD-Security*: `http://teammentordevelopment.wordpress.com/2012/05/19/automated-burp-security-scanning-with-bdd-security/`.

- Webpwnized's video tutorials on Burp Suite: `https://www.youtube.com/results?search_query=burp+webpwnized`.

- *Pentesting Adobe Flex Applications*: `http://blog.gdssecurity.com/storage/presentations/OWASP_NYNJMetro_Pentesting_Flex.pdf`.

- *Pen-testing HSTS (Http Strict Security Transport) Sites with Burp*: `http://superconfigure.wordpress.com/2013/01/29/pen-testing-hsts-http-strict-transport-security-sites-with-burp/`.

Pentesting thick clients

Pentesting thick clients can be done in the following two ways:

- *Pentesting Java Thick Applications with Burp JDSer*: `https://www.netspi.com/blog/entryid/67/pentesting-java-thick-applications-with-burp-jdser`

- *"Reversing" Non-Proxy Aware HTTPS Thick Clients w/ Burp*: `http://blog.spiderlabs.com/2014/02/reversing-non-proxy-aware-https-thick-clients-w-burp.html`

Testing mobile applications for web security using Burp Suite

Some useful resources to test mobile applications for web security using Burp Suite can be found at the following locations:

- *How To Set Up An iOS Pen Testing Environment*: `http://eightbit.io/post/64319534191/how-to-set-up-an-ios-pen-testing-environment`

- *Importing Burp certificate for Android pentesting without root*: `http://backtosecurity.com/importing-burp-certificate-for-android-pentesting-without-root/`

- *Windows 8 Mobile Burp Proxy Setup*: `http://pentest-forum.com/index.php?topic=688.0`

- *Pentesting Web Service with anti CSRF token using BurpPro*: `http://www.notsosecure.com/blog/2014/07/02/pentesting-web-service-with-csrf-token-with-burp-pro/`

- *iOS Assessments with Burp + iFunBox + SQLite*: `http://blog.nvisium.com/2014/08/ios-assessments-with-burp-ifunbox-sqlite.html`

Extensions references

Here are some references with which you can explore the world of extensions:

- **Setting up the environment for Burp Extensions**: Before we can write extensions, we need to ensure that the environment is set up. This is very important if you want to avoid hours and hours of frustration with yourself. More information can be found at `http://www.burpextensions.com/tutorials/setting-up-the-pythonjython-environment-for-burp-suite/`.

- **Writing your first Burp Extension**: A gentle introduction to writing your first extension—use the code provided here as your boiler plate to test whether your environment has been set up properly. If the extension gets added without any errors, then you are good to go. More information can be found at `http://blog.portswigger.net/2012/12/writing-your-first-burp-extension.html`.

- **Write a simple Burp Extension in Python**: Apart from the code given in *Chapter 9, Using Burp Extensions and Writing Your Own*, this has to be the place where you learn how to write a Burp Extension in Python. The code is simple, the post explains all that is required, and the extension will do useful things as soon as it is added. More information can be found at `http://www.burpextensions.com/tutorials/tutorial-python-extension-post-1/` and `http://www.burpextensions.com/downloads/pythontutorial-1.txt`.

- **Burp's official API documentation**: Once you have a working extension with help from the mentioned resources, you will be hungry for more. Now is the time to dive into the Java documentation and start reading it to make the next cool extension. More information can be found at `http://portswigger.net/burp/extender/api/index.html`.

- **Burp Extensions tutorials**: Now that you have read the official documentation, you can make full use of these tutorials that delve deeper into extensions. More information about Burp Extensions tutorials can be found at `http://www.burpextensions.com/category/tutorials/`.

- **Extending Burp Proxy with Extensions**: `http://blog.opensecurityresearch.com/2014/03/extending-burp.html`.

- **Burp Extensions in Burp App Store**: `https://pro.portswigger.net/bappstore/`.

- **Burp Crawljax Selenium JUnit integration**: `https://github.com/malerisch/burp-csj`.

- **Writing and debugging Burp Suite Extensions in Python**: `http://sethsec.blogspot.in/2014/01/writing-and-debugging-burpsuite.html`.

- **Searching GitHub for Burp Extensions**: `https://github.com/search?utf8=%E2%9C%93&q=burp+extension`.

- **Writing Burp Extensions in any language you want**: `https://github.com/liftsecurity/burpbuddy`.

Books

Books that should be part of every web application security tester's library, especially for using Burp Suite:

- If you are a web application penetration tester, you should get the *Web Application Hacker's Handbook, Dafydd Stuttard and Marcus Pinto, Wiley*. This is the de facto book on web application security.

- Get the *Instant Burp Suite Starter, Luca Carettoni, Packt Publishing*, to get started quickly on using Burp Suite.

- *The Tangled Web: A Guide to Securing Modern Web Applications, Michal Zalewski, No Starch Press*. He is the author of the extremely informative *Browser Security Handbook* as well: `https://code.google.com/p/browsersec/wiki/Main`.

Summary

After reading this chapter, you will be really busy. Now, you can fully explore Burp Suite with all the help available to you, including what this book has to offer. You will get a pretty good idea how application testers the world over use Burp Suite in myriad of inventive ways to test applications as attackers. If you are active on Twitter, following the accounts mentioned previously might offer some more references, links, and documentation as well.

The references and links are provided to give you a good overview of how Burp is flexible enough to be extended and utilized in various interesting ways. If you find some great references, do let me know at @makash.

Index

R

rational expression 78
regular expression
  about 78
  online resources 78
  URL 78
Reissue Request scripter 107
Repeater
  about 60
  user interface 60, 61
  using 62
response modification 48
responses
  intercepting 48
Ruby environment
  setting up, for Burp Extensions 98

S

sample analysis, Sequencer 71
Samurai WTF Course Slides
  URL 110
Scanner
  about 57-59
  scanning optimization 59
  scanning requests 59
  URL 59
scan queues 60
scheduled tasks 113, 114
Scope
  and Burp Suite tools 23
  inclusive pattern, versus exclusive
     pattern 24
  out-of-scope requests, dropping 24
  targets adding, ways 22
Search 88, 89
search form 88
Secure Shell Server (SSH) 26
Secure Socket Layer (SSL) 31
Sequencer
  about 67
  sample analysis 71
  test for randomness, of tokens 68-70
  token analysis 70, 71
  URL, for tests 71

SOCKS proxies
  dealing with 25
  SSH tunneling, using as 26, 27
  working with 25
spidering
  overview 63-67
sqlmap 119
SSH tunneling
  using, as SOCK proxy 26, 27
SSL pass-through 35
state
  restoring 110-112
  saving 110-112

T

Target Analyzer tool 90, 91
targets
  adding to Scope, ways 22
  list, loading from file 23
Task Scheduler 93
thick clients, pentesting
  references 120
token analysis, Sequencer 70, 71
Tor browser bundle
  URL 26

U

upstream proxies
  dealing with 25

W

web application security testing, Burp
  about 118
  references 118, 119
web crawling. *See* spidering

About Packt Publishing

Packt, pronounced 'packed', published its first book "*Mastering phpMyAdmin for Effective MySQL Management*" in April 2004 and subsequently continued to specialize in publishing highly focused books on specific technologies and solutions.

Our books and publications share the experiences of your fellow IT professionals in adapting and customizing today's systems, applications, and frameworks. Our solution based books give you the knowledge and power to customize the software and technologies you're using to get the job done. Packt books are more specific and less general than the IT books you have seen in the past. Our unique business model allows us to bring you more focused information, giving you more of what you need to know, and less of what you don't.

Packt is a modern, yet unique publishing company, which focuses on producing quality, cutting-edge books for communities of developers, administrators, and newbies alike. For more information, please visit our website: www.packtpub.com.

Writing for Packt

We welcome all inquiries from people who are interested in authoring. Book proposals should be sent to author@packtpub.com. If your book idea is still at an early stage and you would like to discuss it first before writing a formal book proposal, contact us; one of our commissioning editors will get in touch with you.

We're not just looking for published authors; if you have strong technical skills but no writing experience, our experienced editors can help you develop a writing career, or simply get some additional reward for your expertise.

Building Virtual Pentesting Labs for Advanced Penetration Testing

ISBN: 978-1-78328-477-1   Paperback: 430 pages

Build intricate virtual architecture to practice any penetration testing technique virtually

1. Build and enhance your existing pentesting methods and skills.

2. Get a solid methodology and approach to testing.

3. Step-by-step tutorials helping you build complex virtual architecture.

Learning Nessus for Penetration Testing

ISBN: 978-1-78355-099-9   Paperback: 116 pages

Master how to perform IT infrastructure security vulnerability assessments using Nessus with tips and insights from real-world challenges faced during vulnerability assessment

1. Understand the basics of vulnerability assessment and penetration testing as well as the different types of testing.

2. Successfully install Nessus and configure scanning options.

3. Learn useful tips based on real-world issues faced during scanning.

Please check **www.PacktPub.com** for information on our titles

PUBLISHING

**Penetration Testing
with BackBox**

An introductory guide to performing crucial penetration testing operations using BackBox

Stefan Umit Uygur

Penetration Testing with BackBox

ISBN: 978-1-78328-297-5   Paperback: 130 pages

An introductory guide to performing crucial penetration testing operations using BackBox

1. Experience the real world of penetration testing with BackBox Linux using live, practical examples.

2. Gain an insight into auditing and penetration testing processes by reading though live sessions.

3. Learn how to carry out your own testing using the latest techniques and methodologies.

**Metasploit Penetration
Testing Cookbook**
Second Edition

Over 80 recipes to master the most widely used penetration testing framework

Monika Agarwal
Abhinav Singh

Metasploit Penetration Testing Cookbook

Second Edition

ISBN: 978-1-78216-678-8   Paperback: 320 pages

Over 80 recipes to master the most widely used penetration testing framework

1. Special focus on the latest operating systems, exploits, and penetration testing techniques for wireless, VOIP, and cloud.

2. This book covers a detailed analysis of third-party tools based on the Metasploit framework to enhance the penetration testing experience.

3. Detailed penetration testing techniques for different specializations such as wireless networks, VOIP systems, along with a brief introduction to penetration testing in the cloud.

Please check **www.PacktPub.com** for information on our titles